MW00794957

LED *by the*
HAND *of* CHRIST

LED *by the*
HAND *of* CHRIST

By SUZANNE FREEMAN
As told to Shirley Bahlmann

spring creek
BOOK COMPANY
Provo, Utah

© 2004 Suzanne Freeman and Shirley Bahlmann
All Rights Reserved.

ISBN: 1-932898-25-5

e. 1

Published by:

Spring Creek Book Company

P.O. Box 50355

Provo, Utah 84605-0355

Cover design © Spring Creek Book Company

Cover design by Nicole Cunningham

Cover painting by Rhett E. Murray

Printed in the United States of America

10 9 8 7 6 5 4 3 2 1

Printed on acid-free paper

Library of Congress Cataloging-in-Publication Data

Freeman, Suzanne (Suzanne Scholes)

 Led by the hand of Christ / by Suzanne Freeman ; as told to Shirley
Bahlmann.

  p. cm.

 Summary: "The author describes a near-death experience (NDE)
she experienced while having a miscarriage during an ectopic
pregnancy"--Provided by publisher.

 ISBN 1-932898-25-5 (pbk. : alk. paper)

 1. Near-death experiences--Religious aspects--Christianity. 2.
Freeman, Suzanne (Suzanne Scholes) I. Bahlmann, Shirley. II. Title.

 BT833.F74 2004

 277.3'0829'092--dc22

                              2004022844

Dedication

I dedicate this book to the Lord,
my Savior, Jesus Christ.

Acknowledgments

To my true love and soul mate, James, for his understanding and patience. Together we have shared many happy times, many hard times, and our children, who make us complete: Christy, Coreena, Kyle, Connie, Luke, Cody, Lance, Wesley, and Joseph Porter. I love them with all my heart and they are my reason for living. I am grateful every day for my eternal family.

To Linda, Ranae, Denise and Natalie; thanks for guiding me on my journey of truth and light.

To Shirley; thanks for your gift of words. You write what is in my heart.

Thanks also to Melinda Roth R.N. and DellRay Anderson M.D. for medical information.

Introduction

To me, the words "near death" seem too harsh. When I hear the saying, it seems to mean "stopped living." This is far from the truth. We don't stop living, because death is not the end. We move on, like graduating from high school in order to go to a higher place to learn. I prefer "nearly passed on," or "near passing," or even "spirit vacation!"

Through this experience I have learned that our loved ones that have passed are not far from us. I know my visit to the other side was tailored for me, with experiences that I needed to continue my life on earth. I know that others have had separate experiences. I share mine because I feel that others may be helped by something they read here. I have personally learned many things from the other side. Everyday things aren't as important as they were before August 1999.

I used to feel that I would not live to be old, but hoped it would be after all my children were raised. I certainly did not think that I would ever have the grand adventure of seeing the other side and live to tell the tale. The hardest part was coming back. Heaven is a place of peace and rest. Who wouldn't want that? But I knew my children needed me.

The most important thing in my life now is family, because that is what matters most in heaven, not a fancy car or how many square feet your house has. We can't take any of that with us. Having one eye on the Lord and the other on Heavenly Father is what will bring us back to them. Then we can build our mansions on high.

It is not always easy to share spiritual experiences. My only hope in sharing mine is that it will touch many lives and give hope to those who grieve for a loved one. For this reason, I give it to the world. I do not take my experience for granted. I cherish it deeply and hope that through sharing it, it will bring you peace and understanding. I pray that the Lord's spirit will be with you as you read this book.

With my love,

Suzanne

Foreword

In the peace of the night, I sometimes get lost somewhere between dreamland and reality. It is then when my memories meet me. Small chapters from childhood will dance with me down the path of time. The smell of bread begs me to follow.

I remember my mom baking bread on a rainy day. She always said, "This is the best time to make bread."

The sound of the mixer would bring all of the kids running to help. Mom would give each of us little tasks that made us feel important, but kept us out of the way.

When the dough was all mixed and ready for the pans, Mom would give us each a big pinch of dough. We would hold our little hands out to see whose piece was bigger.

Cori would chant, "Mine is bigger than yours!"

I would stick my tongue out and say, "Nuh-uh!"

Kyle would have his mouth full of dough. This left him out of the contest.

Mom had small bread pans she passed out. I tried to get mine to look like Mom's, gently molding each loaf into shape. I tried to match her, but portions of it would get eaten too fast.

When all was done, Mom's bread loaves would turn out golden brown. My loaves would be hard and look like a moon rock.

Soon the melody of the dance would change. Songs of bedtime still sing memorable notes in my head. My dad would tuck me in at night, something I always looked forward to. He would check for monsters and other unwanted things.

Dad then said, "Did you say your prayers?"

I would beg him to stay and say them with me. In my prayers I would ask Father in Heaven to bless me to sleep good, and that no monsters would come into my dreams. By this time, I was ready for bed.

As time passed, my bedtime prayer would not be enough. I got lazy, and my dreams got worse. Monsters found a way to break the chains of prayer.

On Easter, I got a painting of Christ. That night, I hung it up in my room. The nightmares stopped. Because of this big success I began a Christ painting collection.

Dad and Mom always believed that you should have a picture of Christ in every room. That is something I knew my parents both had—a love for Christ. That love shone in their eyes. At just the mention of Christ, my mom glows with joy. Such closeness to the Savior is just one of a number of gifts he gives us.

God gives gifts out of love. "For God so loved the world, that he gave his only begotten son, that whosoever believeth in him should not perish, but have everlasting life." (John 3:16) This scripture by itself rings heavenly bells in my soul. It gives me an understanding of my mom's gift.

Christ likes to give parables to teach or explain. This is my parable:

On a table is a gift. The brightly colored wrapping catches an unexpected eye. Suzie knows who the gift is for, right from the beginning. Thoughts of, "Oh, I can't!" or "That can't be for me," enter her mind. As fast as the thoughts come, they depart just as quickly. Suzie picks up the gift and opens the box. What she finds inside is more gorgeous and beautiful than the outside. The gentle whispering then hits her like a ton of bricks. "Share what I gave you."

That is what my mom is doing with you. She is sharing her sacred gift. It is my hope that you will enjoy and love it, too.

When the time comes to wake up, my heart drops. Before I awaken from my dreams and join the world again, I would like to end with a thought from my heart: I know my Savior loves me. I'm thankful for all that he gives me. I can see his love with all the bright beauty in the world. I'm grateful for my love for him. I don't know what I would do without it.

If you are reading this, dear Savior, I would just like to say, "I love you, too."

Thanks for all,

Christy Freeman

CHAPTER 1

What's Wrong With Me?

I knew I was pregnant, even though all the tests said I wasn't. Believe me, after bearing seven children in fourteen years, I knew what being pregnant felt like.

Still, every time a test came back negative, I had the disquieting sense of a child waking up on a school morning feeling just awful, and telling my mother I was too sick to go to school.

"You don't look sick," the mother in my mind would say, narrowing her eyes at me. "Let's take your temperature."

I opened my mouth for the thermometer, certain I'd be vindicated, only to have it pulled out after the required three minutes and Mom squinting at the impossibly thin line of mercury with a frown on her face.

"You don't have a fever," she would say. "Now stop playing sick and get to school."

My heart drooped and I shuffled off with my arms wrapped around my aching tummy, knowing in my heart of hearts that I was going to throw up and hoping that it wouldn't happen during lunch.

Yet even without a positive pregnancy test, my own inner knowing assured me that I was carrying a baby. My mother's intuition boosted my hope and accelerated the anticipation of soon being able to feel my little one move inside me.

I wondered if we were having a boy or a girl. Maybe it would be twins again. I already had a set of twin boys, so I imagined how fun it would be to have twin girls. It didn't matter to me what we had, I was just thrilled to be having another baby. I even pulled out my maternity clothes, taking courage from knowing that in spite of what the tests said, in eight months I'd have a sweet little baby to prove my claim. I didn't doubt it for an instant.

Then, one morning in August of 1999, my husband James said, "Hey, Suz, do you want to go to Orem with me?"

I hesitated. In spite of the never-ending laundry and household chores that naturally go along with a large family, I was sorely tempted to leave our oldest daughter in charge of the little ones for a few hours and enjoy some time alone with James.

"What are you driving?" I asked.

"The Toyota," he said.

My hopes for a pleasant trip in the family van crumbled into a sad heap of disappointment, although it didn't make sense to drive the gas-guzzling van if it would be just the two of us going.

Yet making the 50-mile drive in our old Toyota truck—equipped with shock absorbers that were only there in spirit—made me think twice. James might as well have pulled those useless things off completely. The only thing they were good for was to send a jolt from every bump in the road right through the cab and into the passengers. We would be human shock absorbers for the duration of the trip.

Still, I hadn't been able to spend much time with James lately, since he worked as an over-the-road driver. I really did feel that a break from my regular routine would boost my spirits. So after checking with 14-year-old Christy, and finding her willing to tend her younger siblings, I told James I would go.

We buckled ourselves into the ugly, yet dependable, old truck and headed north. Every bump or divot in the road sent a jolt right up through the seat. I hung onto the truck handle and wondered how a paved road that looked so smooth could hide so many nefarious bumps. Every single bounce made me more determined that no matter how well the truck ran, I was all for trading it in the moment we reached the city.

We couldn't get there fast enough for me. As soon as we pulled into the computer store parking lot, I popped out of the seat and stood up, welcoming the solid pavement beneath my feet. I eyed James over the hood of the truck and said, "Honey, either we're going to trade this truck in, or else I've got to get a pillow for me to sit on for the ride home. If we don't, all that will be left of me is a pile of rattling bones."

James shrugged. "I'm afraid that this truck has a trade-in value of about zero. We'll get a pillow."

We'd only been shopping a short time when, without any warning, severe pain stabbed my left side and zipped around through my abdomen.

"Ow!" I cried, instantly covering the ache with both hands. Why had it taken me until now to remember that this was the very truck that I'd ridden in at six months pregnant with one of our older children, a ride that had ended with me going into labor? The Toyota was not a pregnancy-friendly truck, and the lapse in memory was further proof that I was dealing with some hormonal loopholes.

"Suzie!" James said, concern traced in every line of his face. "Are you all right?"

"It hurts," I managed to gasp, standing perfectly still and trying to remember how to breathe.

He stared at my hands covering my abdomen. "But you had your appendix out last year," he said, his voice pleading, trying to reason with the pain.

"I . . . know . . . that," I panted, not bothering to keep the impatience out of my voice.

"Come on, Suzie, I've got to get you to a doctor." James held my shoulder and exerted gentle pressure on my back until I made a move toward the exit.

I took one step and nearly collapsed against my husband. The pain was incredible. *This is ridiculous,* I told myself, but it didn't make any difference to the pain. I gritted my teeth. Why had I come, anyway? I should have stayed home. Yet the drive in the truck hadn't been any worse than an amusement ride my kids might have convinced me to try, and I was only in the first month of pregnancy. It hadn't crossed my mind that anything I rode in at this stage would make a bit of difference.

Well, it was too late to go back and do it over now. I groaned in frustration. "It hurts to walk."

"You can't stay here," James said. "Just take it slow." He pulled me in to lean against him.

Normally, I'm not one who runs to doctors for every little ache and pain. I prefer to do my own doctoring, but every nerve ending in my body cried out that this was an emergency.

James drove me to the Instacare facility in Lindon, a town just north of Orem. After taking my vital statistics, the staff gave me a pregnancy test. When they returned with the results, the little girl inside me shrank back, fully expecting to hear that she wasn't sick enough to stay home from school.

"You're pregnant," the nurse said, a smile of congratulations on her face. "We're sending you to the American Fork Hospital for an ultrasound."

My heart lifted, then soared. At last, the test had come back positive, proving what I already knew. After I told my family, I'd let my good friend Pam know that I would be having a baby just one month after hers, with the test to back up my claim. Now I could tell everyone that I was pregnant. I had proof.

It was a perfectly wonderful, perfectly normal condition that had just been aggravated by a bumpy ride in an old truck, that's all. _Everything would turn out fine_, I told myself. I'd done this six times before— including once with the twins—and there was absolutely nothing to worry about.

James smiled down at me, his eyes alight, as happy to find out we were having our eighth child as he had been with our first. I smiled back, because we had no idea what trials still lay before us.

James drove me to the hospital in high spirits, trying to guess the baby's due date and whether it would be a boy or girl. I listened to him and offered an occasional comment, my arms wrapped around my mid-section as snugly as the joy wrapped around my heart.

In happy anticipation, I endured the light pressure of the ultrasound device on my sore stomach, watching and waiting to catch the first glimpse of our miniature child enlarged on the ultrasound screen. I knew it was too soon to tell, but I had the feeling that it was a little girl. Maybe it was because all three of my daughters had been born here in the American Fork Hospital, but it didn't really matter. I simply longed to see whatever there was of my baby. Perhaps I'd be able to see the heart beating. My throat clogged with emotion. Hearing the miraculous sound of my babies' heartbeats for the first time always made me cry.

The technician moved the handheld device across my abdomen, from side to side and back again. I stared at the screen, not familiar enough with my insides to know just what I was seeing amid the shifting gray mass on the monitor. I kept waiting for the technician to stop and say, "There it is."

He didn't stop. He never said, "There it is." Instead, after what seemed a long time, he turned to me and said, "I'm sorry, I can't find anything."

My heart squeezed in bitter disappointment and tears burned the back of my eyes. Whether rational or not, all I could think of was that the stupid truck had done it again. The ride must have put me into labor, only this time the baby was far too small to save.

I was miscarrying our baby.

CHAPTER 2

Ectopic

I'm sorry," the doctor said. "A combination of factors leads me to believe that you have an ectopic pregnancy."

I was too stunned to speak. Apparently, so was my husband.

The doctor went on, "Your lack of positive results on earlier pregnancy tests, the type of pain you're describing, and no conclusive findings with the ultrasound are all symptoms indicative of an ectopic pregnancy."

James found his voice and finally asked, "What exactly is that?"

The doctor turned somber eyes on James. "It's when an embryo starts to grow in a place other than the uterus."

"How can that be?" I managed to blurt out. I had never heard of such a thing and couldn't imagine how it could possibly happen.

The doctor leaned forward and clasped his hands together. "In an ectopic pregnancy, instead of traveling to the uterus, the embryo generally attaches itself inside one of the fallopian tubes and starts to grow. Without surgery, the tube could burst and cause serious internal bleeding. On rare occasions, the fertilized egg will escape the reproductive system altogether, eventually attaching itself to another organ such as the liver, the spleen, or even to the outside of the uterus."

I felt dizzy, my head swirling with images of a pregnant Arnold Schwarzenegger in the movie comedy, *Junior*. I'd found it hilarious when a male researcher implanted a human embryo in his own abdominal cavity, then went through the whole nine months with symptoms that mirrored my own experiences with pregnancy. He ultimately had a C-Section, delivered a healthy baby, and everyone lived happily ever after.

Would I have a happy ending, too?

"Is it serious?" James glanced at me with a quick, anxious appraisal, then turned back to the doctor. "What's going to happen to her?"

The doctor straightened in his chair and put his hands on his knees. "No one can say for sure what will happen. In rare cases, an ectopic pregnancy may resolve itself on its own and reabsorb, but in almost every case, surgery is required to remove the embryo and stop the bleeding."

"But you aren't absolutely sure that's what it is?" I asked, unconsciously placing my hand over my abdomen as if that would protect my tiny baby from the hopeless scenario that the doctor had just painted for us.

The doctor shook his head, but without enthusiasm. "We weren't able to locate the embryo."

I couldn't stop the tears from welling up in my eyes. "Does riding in a truck without shock absorbers make it worse?"

His eyes widened. "That doesn't make any difference. The situation was set the moment the embryo implanted itself in the wrong place." Then he held my gaze. "I suggest that you go straight home and see your own doctor. If the growth bursts the fallopian tube, it would cause internal bleeding."

He then leaned forward as if to drive the point home. "And if the pain gets worse, go to the hospital immediately."

I almost wanted to laugh at his absurd comment, because riding in that old Toyota would most certainly make my pain worse, but I couldn't laugh. My throat was too full of disappointment.

James walked with me to the truck, his earlier joy swallowed up by our shared sorrow. As soon as I sat down and slammed the door shut, I said, "I want to visit Mom and Dad."

"But the doctor said go straight home," James protested.

"They're only a few minutes from here, and it won't make any difference to the baby." I choked on a sob, then swallowed. "We might as well stop by." I reached up and brushed a tear away.

James reached over and squeezed my hand. "Aw, Suzie," he muttered, grief in every syllable.

We drove in silence to my parent's house in American Fork. To my surprise, both of my sisters were there.

"Suzie!" Merrianne said as soon as she saw me. She wrapped her arms around me. "What a nice surprise! I'm so glad you're here. Now I can tell you the good news, too." She looked around at the family circle, her face alight. "I'm pregnant!"

Her announcement twisted a knife in my heart, tearing it open wide enough for my sad story to spill out.

My family listened to all I had to say, then Merrianne patted my back. "Well, the doctor did say it could resolve itself."

"And he also said it was just symptoms," my sister Ruth Ann chimed in. "He didn't say he knew for sure. Maybe it's one of those times where if you get enough bed rest, you'll be able to keep it."

"Yes," Merrianne agreed, her face glowing. "It would

be so fun to have our babies at the same time so they can grow up with a cousin just their age."

I couldn't have agreed with her more.

The ache in my heart had been lessened by sharing our situation with my family. After staying long enough to have supper with my sisters and parents, James drove me home. I arrived in one piece, but exhausted and heartsick. I made my way to my bedroom with a wake of little children following along behind, all trying to talk at once. I hugged the closest ones, appreciating the precious feel of their soft little bodies—the young, velvety skin under my hands and the wispy hair that brushed my cheek when I bent to embrace them.

I collapsed onto my bed and listened for as long as it took for all of them tell me about how they'd spent their time while Mom and Dad were gone. Their voices would have been all the sweeter if they'd been accompanied by an infant's cry, a sound I realized I might not get to hear again in our home.

CHAPTER 3

Emergency Measures

I decided to put myself on bed rest to see if by some miracle I could save the little baby that I carried within me. I couldn't see how it would make any difference if I didn't go see my doctor right away. He'd still be there later if I needed him.

"Bed rest" is a relative term when you have seven children and a husband who works as a long distance trucker. Still, as I allowed myself a greater part of each day to lie in bed, the pain seemed to lessen. My yearning for the baby I still carried within me blossomed, willing it to stay and grow, to be born healthy so we could all welcome it into our family. Since there were no outward signs of a miscarriage, I hoped that maybe the doctor was wrong, that it wasn't ectopic, and that somehow I might keep this baby. I was determined to be as careful as possible in order to give this little one every chance.

A few days after James went back on the road as

a security guard driving an armored truck for Brink's Company, the pain inside me swelled to greater proportions.

With the children who kept running into my bedroom with near-constant needs, and the increasing pain no matter how much I rested, I decided that it was useless to prolong the inevitable. I'd get up out of bed and go about my business, letting nature take its course, even though my heart ached with impending loss. It didn't matter that I hadn't carried this little one for very long, I was still emotionally attached to the tiny life within me.

One morning I decided it would do me good to walk the four blocks to the Post Office to get our mail. We live in a small rural town in central Utah called Spring City, a beautiful little place where we can leave our doors unlocked without worry, where people wave at each other when they pass on the streets, a town so small that it doesn't even deliver door-to-door mail.

The walk was longer than I remembered it. I was huffing and puffing before I even got there. I knew I was out of shape, but certainly not so much as to be worn out by walking only four blocks.

By the time I arrived at my destination, it was all I could do to retrieve the mail. I felt so weak that I knew I couldn't make it home. From the Post Office steps, I faced the church across the street. The shade from the trees surrounding the church beckoned to me, inviting me to rest under the canopy of leaves.

I managed to make it across the street on shaking legs before I crumpled onto the south steps of the church house. I wiped the sweat from my brow with the back of my hand, avoided any pressure on the tender spot in my abdomen, and concentrated on breathing slowly. What I really wanted to do was collapse onto the grass and let myself go limp, but I didn't have the courage to stretch out alongside Main Street where everyone could see me. I sat and breathed and did my best to gather my strength for the journey home.

Thirty minutes later, I thought that maybe I could make it. I pushed myself to my feet and started back at the only speed I had: slow. It was difficult to even pick one foot up and move it ahead of the other. Once that was accomplished, I had to make myself do it again, and again, and again. Whenever a car drove past, I stared at it with envy, wishing that I were sitting inside. Most of them were driven by people I knew, friends who gave me a cheery wave before disappearing down the road.

I wanted a ride so badly that I thought about sticking my arm out, calling to them, and begging to be taken home. Yet when it came right down to it, I couldn't make myself do it. I was less than three blocks away. What would they think of me, asking for a ride for three blocks? I didn't want anyone to think I was lazy, so even though my heart pounded with the effort of moving one slow step after the other, and even though my soul cried out, *Please take me home,* I remained silent.

After what felt like close to eternity, I finally made it to my front door. I worked my way through the house and into my bedroom where I collapsed onto my bed in an exhausted heap.

A couple of nights later, I was jerked awake by a sharp pain that sliced into my left side and shot down my leg with relentless fury. I panicked. The doctor in Provo had told me to go the hospital if the pain got worse, and this was, without question, worse. But James was on the road, and I didn't dare drive myself in the condition I was in. There was no one else at home who could drive me, and I wasn't about to call anyone in the middle of the night. The thought of disturbing my neighbors worried me almost as much as the awful pain inside of me.

I managed to drag myself to the bathroom and fumbled in the medicine cabinet until I found some over-the-counter pain reliever. I swallowed three of the pills, then stood with a death grip on the sink until the pain subsided enough that I could make my way back to bed.

The next morning I was so tired, it seemed as if

I was surrounded by a thin fog that garbled people's words and made it hard to see clearly. I didn't hurt as much anymore, and it seemed like too much trouble to go to the doctor.

My eyelids kept sinking down over my eyes, and every time I sat down I nodded off toward sleep. My children were frustrated with me, vying for my attention, but it seemed as if they were far away, even when they stood right beside me. It was a frustrating situation for all of us.

Trying to do any work in the house was difficult. If I did the dishes I'd need to rest. One load of laundry would sap all my energy. Besides mourning the loss of my unborn baby, I figured that my body was weary from the process of miscarrying. When a baby is conceived, the natural thing for a body to do is to grow and nourish it until it's time to be born. But this child would never see the light of day, and it felt like my body was mourning the loss, too.

The next morning I woke up hurting worse than anything I'd felt so far. I swallowed more pain pills from my dwindling supply, realizing that I couldn't put off my visit to the doctor any longer. By now, I just wished the miscarriage would get over with. If I wasn't going to be able to have this baby to cuddle against my neck and smell the sweet new-baby smell of its hair, to pat its tiny back or slide my thumb across its miniature toes when I changed its diaper, to wash and fold the impossibly small sleepers and booties while the baby slumbered in its carrier, then I just wanted to get it over with. I wanted to stop wondering what it would look like, and whether it might be twins. I wanted to get on with taking care of the children I already had without battling the increasingly constant ache of my body and the tearing sadness of my soul.

I blinked back tears and bent over to pick a towel up off the floor. My eyes flew open wide and I stifled a scream as pain as sharp as a tornado of broken glass tore through my belly.

"Oh, oh, oh, no," I gasped as I staggered toward the telephone. I wished with all my heart that James were with me. I needed him in the worst way, but he wasn't back yet. He was still on the road, doing his best to provide for us. The rising agony inside of me joined with the anxiety of being separated from my husband when I needed him so desperately, increasing my misery. What could I do now?

CHAPTER 4

The Longest Wait

Imade my way to the phone and dialed my sister Ruth Ann's number from memory. Hunched over from pain, tears rolling down my cheeks, I listened to the phone on the other end of the line ring and ring and ring. *Please be there*, I begged silently. I honestly doubted that I had enough strength to dial again. Then I heard the receiver click.

"Hello?" My brother-in-law, Wayne, said into the phone.

My throat clogged up with tears and I gripped the receiver with both hands. "Wayne," I said, then choked on a sob.

"What's wrong, Suzie?" Wayne asked, instantly concerned.

"You've got to come and take me to the hospital," I begged.

There was a moment of shocked silence. "Haven't you been to see your doctor yet?" he demanded.

I knew that Ruth Ann had told Wayne about my condition. I also knew that one of his friends had died from an ectopic pregnancy.

"No."

"Why not?" His voice was a shout, and I shrank into myself, even though I knew that he was only hollering at me because he was concerned.

Fresh tears burned in my eyes. "I wanted to try to keep it," I mumbled.

There was an instant of silence before Wayne said, "Suzie, I'm in Provo and you're in Spring City. There's no way that you can wait an hour and a half for me to come and get you. You've got to call a friend or neighbor for a ride to the Emergency Room right now."

My heart sank in despair, and I rubbed at my wet eyes with a knuckle. I felt so stupid. Why had I even called my sister, who lived so far away, in the first place? It didn't make any sense, unless you took into consideration that I was completely desperate and in terrible pain.

"What will I do with my kids?" I asked.

"I don't know," Wayne answered, the agitation in his voice apparent. "Here, talk to Ruth Ann, but get to the hospital right away, will you?" Without waiting for an answer, Wayne was gone.

A moment later, my sister was on the phone. "Suzie?"

New tears wet my cheeks at the sound of my sister's voice. "I've got to go to the hospital," I wailed. "I hurt so bad. I don't want it to be, but I must be having an ectopic pregnancy like the doctor said." My words drowned in a sob, and I began weeping.

Ruth Ann had worked for Sheriff dispatch 911, and was taught to treat any woman of child-bearing age with severe pain as an emergency. "Suzie, how much blood is there?" she demanded.

Her brisk question pulled me out of the mire of self-pity and I wiped my eyes with the back of my hand. "Not much," I answered.

"How much?"

"It's really light, there's almost nothing there."

"I'm leaving right now," Ruth Ann said. "Christy can watch the other children until I get there. Who can you call to take you to the hospital?"

Out of the panic battling with the pain inside me emerged a warm reassurance that my children would be just fine if I left them alone to go to the hospital. Ruth Ann's no-nonsense voice on the other end of the line helped me to get a clear mental picture of what I needed to do. Her words infused me with enough strength and determination that I knew I could take the next step. Everything was going to be all right.

"Yes, my friend Pam can probably give me a ride," I answered. "I'll call her now."

Pam was home when I called, and answered on the first ring. She agreed to come right over. I hung up the phone and moved to the front door to wait.

In a desperate bid to alleviate some of my suffering, I concentrated on the first time I'd caught sight of James across the church gymnasium at a ward Christmas party. He was, quite literally, a dream come true. Stars did cartwheels in my head and butterflies danced in my stomach as I recognized the man I had seen in my dreams so many times. My seventeen-year-old heart pounded in anticipation, and I couldn't stop staring at him sitting there in the American Fork Fifth Ward, fresh from the mission field and as handsome as all get out. Sparks flew. It was love at first sight, and I determined then and there that James Freeman would soon feel the same way about me, if he didn't already. This was the man I was going to marry.

It didn't bother me a bit that I was still in high school, probably because I didn't have what you would necessarily call an idyllic childhood. I never felt like I could relate well to other kids, the ones who raised their hands in class all the time and those who read through a book like it was easy. It was even sometimes hard to relate to my own brothers and sisters, because I had dyslexia at a time when educators still weren't sure what it was.

The ironic thing is that I was the fourth child born

to my parents in four years, and they told me that when I was two years old, I could get into things faster than my older siblings. My parents came to the conclusion that I was probably a little bit smarter than the others, so when I got into school and had a hard time reading, it really surprised them.

In first grade, I was put in a special education program. In spite of the extra help, I still struggled with math and reading, so Mom and Dad had the school hold me back a year. I did better the second time around, and the summer after my repeat of first grade, my Grandma Scholes visited the school and talked them into letting me skip ahead to third grade.

I know she meant well, but missing the instruction that went along with the second grade year put me even further behind when I again found myself in a class with my peers. I had almost no friends in elementary school. Besides the stigma of being a special education kid, I wasn't dressed in the latest fashions, and my hair wasn't always combed or fixed nicely.

In third grade, my teacher didn't understand me or how to help me overcome my stumbling blocks to learning. She actually told me that I was too stupid to do the work. Her method of dealing with me was to hand me a picture book and leave me to my own devices. I spent most of my third grade year staring out the window.

One day, I made a paper pumpkin that was stuffed with newspaper. I hadn't bothered to write my name on it, so when Mrs. Mortenson found it she held it up and in a voice as nice as pie with whipped cream on top, she said, "What a nice pumpkin! Who made this?"

Several of the children answered, "Suzie did."

Mrs. Morrison's face creased in vexation, and without another word she threw the pumpkin at me and turned away.

Even before this incident, I was an intuitive child and could tell who liked me and who didn't. They didn't have to say a word. I just knew. For some reason that I still don't understand, I actually did my best to make adults not like me.

Whatever the reason, for the most part I was pretty much ignored, so I quit trying. I mean, where's the incentive when I, as a fifth grader, could not read as well as my sister in first grade? The message I got loud and clear was that I was too dumb to understand anyway, so why bother?

When I reached sixth grade, I finally made a friend in Carma, and we kept our friendship all through high school.

It was during my high school years when a teacher finally got through to me. She took the time to read exciting books aloud to our class. I was riveted by the adventure that rolled off the pages, and I finally realized that a book could be fun to read instead of drudgery. That experience gave me the impetus to delve into reading with renewed determination.

Throughout my frustrating school years, the only bright ray of hope I could cling to was that I knew my father would champion my cause. On numerous occasions he headed for the school, every time he felt that there was something he could say or do to help my situation. It was a matter of importance to me that he would step in and speak up for me, since all my brothers and sisters were doing well in school and needed no parental intervention.

It would have been simpler for Dad to tell me to shape up and get to work, but somehow he knew I was doing the best I could. In spite of a situation that he didn't fully understand, Dad proved to me that he thought I was worth standing up for, which helped me feel a little better about myself. Dad always believed in me.

Four of my siblings became engineers and one became an emergency medical dispatcher, while I became a wife and mother. I am a creative person in my own right, but I tend toward more kinesthetic pursuits, such as inventing my own recipes and quilting. I do more "hands-on" than "hi-tech" projects. Yet because of my Dad and my high school teacher—and my own determination—I do enjoy reading on occasion.

It didn't bother me one bit to leave the frustrations of school behind and delve into daydreams of becoming Mrs. James Freeman. James eventually caught the same vision I had of our inevitable future together, and we were married on October 14, 1983. My young age didn't seem to bother my parents. When I later asked my mother how she could approve my getting married at seventeen, she said that she had prayed and felt that it was right.

James and I took delight in the arrival of each one of our babies, but now, facing the loss of our eighth child, James wasn't here with me. Standing by the front door with my vision going blurry from the pain, I knew that I needed help immediately, and I missed James desperately.

As soon as Pam drove up to my house, I made my way out to her car with slow steps, trying not to move my body any more than necessary. I was grateful to see that she'd driven her car. There was no way I could have climbed up onto the high seat of a van or truck. I would have passed out from pain.

I lowered myself into the car and sat hunched in misery, only turning my head and lifting my hand to wave at the little faces pressed against our living room window as my children watched me drive away.

Even though Pam's shock absorbers worked perfectly, every little bump or turn hurt me more than

I would have ever thought possible. The ride to the Sanpete Valley Hospital seemed to take forever, when in reality it was a little more than four miles.

I shuffled into the hospital, Pam keeping a slow, measured pace beside me. It was hard to sit down, it was hard to stand up, it was hard to walk or do anything with a body that felt as tender and sore as a giant bruise.

I told the hospital staff that I thought I was miscarrying. They took a urine sample and my blood pressure before getting me ready for a pelvic exam.

Now, with seven childbirths already, you can bet I'm no stranger to pelvic exams. And while they're not my favorite thing in the world to spend my free time doing, ranking right up there with singing "Don't Rain on My Parade" in a bathing suit on Main Street, I knew they were part of the package deal that went along with having babies. In my present condition, though, even lying on my back was terribly uncomfortable. Still, it was the next step toward freeing myself from this constant pain.

I thought I knew what to expect, but I was wholly unprepared for the jolt of sudden pain that sliced through me as soon as I was touched, as if I'd been stabbed with a lightning bolt that started a fire hot enough to melt steel. I screamed and screamed, more hurt twisting inside me than with all the hard labor I'd suffered with any of my children. Mount Vesuvius was exploding in my gut. I writhed and squirmed, trying to sit up, to somehow wrench myself free from the horrible pain.

Somewhere in my agony-fogged brain came the memory of something I'd heard about the human body shutting itself down when it suffers too much pain to endure. My shut-off switch must have been broken, because I remained conscious, even though I would rather have been knocked into deep, dark, senseless oblivion until my body didn't hurt any more.

One nurse glanced at me with disdain, her eyebrows raised high in disapproval. "You'd think someone was having a baby in here," she said as though reprimanding a child who was throwing a tantrum.

Her cold words stabbed my heart. I couldn't believe what she'd said. For one thing, the emotional pain of losing a baby, no matter how far along you are, is very real. For another thing, it sounded as if she were belittling my pain, when she had no idea what I was feeling.

I looked at her standing above me, completely pain-free in her young, healthy body, and wondered if she'd ever even had a child. I wanted to tell her that I had gone through labor with twins, and even though I hadn't had an epidural or any other pain-killer with six of the seven children I'd borne, I was saying "please" and "thank you" throughout the labor and delivery. I could handle pain. I wanted to ask her if she'd like to trade places, if she thought she could bear what I was going through without screaming.

I thought they taught compassion in nursing school, but she must have been absent that day. No one knows how someone feels unless they have been through it themselves.

"We'd better order an ultrasound," someone said.

"How long will that take?" I asked, biting my lip against the pain.

"We've got to wait for a machine, but it should only take a couple of hours." At that time, the rural hospital used a traveling ultrasound machine and technician. I was moved from the emergency room to a regular room to wait.

"I've got to use the bathroom," I announced as soon as I was settled on the bed.

"No, you can't, you've got to have a full bladder in order to have an effective ultrasound reading."

"I can't wait two hours," I said, easing myself off the bed. "I've got to go now."

When I entered the bathroom, I caught sight of myself in the mirror. I hardly recognized the pinched-face woman who stared back at me. I am generally a happy person, but at that moment there was no hint of the dimples that came easily when I smiled, unless those long, saggy lines in my cheeks were them in disguise. The woman in the mirror wore haunted eyes and features so sad that I could hardly look at her, so I dropped my gaze to the reflection of my stomach.

Sad to say, after carrying seven children, my stomach had lost most of its youthful elastic exuberance. Even so, it was easier to look at than my woebegone face, so that's where my eyes migrated.

I didn't know why I'd even bothered to move my sore body into the bathroom, as there was precious little to get rid of since the urine sample I'd given on my arrival. Still, I wasn't going to admit to the nurses that it hadn't been worth the trip.

I made my way back to the bed and sat down, trying to find the least painful position to wait in. About fifteen minutes later, my need to use the bathroom had again reared its impatient head and refused to be ignored. "I've got to use the bathroom," I said.

"You can't! You only went fifteen minutes ago."

"I can't help it. I've got to go."

"You have to have a full bladder for the ultrasound to be most effective. You'll have to wait."

I sat and waited and jiggled my knee. My anger grew in proportion to the urge that swelled inside me. I had to void my bladder. It was not a matter of just holding it in, I was in actual pain. I had to use the bathroom, whether it made sense to the nurses or not, and I was going. Who was I to deny the urgent pressure within me? It's like saying that Niagara isn't a waterfall. Even though my brain told my body it was ridiculous to have to go again, my body was in no mood to listen.

"I can't wait," I said, and tip-toed into the bathroom, trying to step lightly enough that I didn't wake up any more pain. I avoided the stranger in the mirror and took care of business, which frankly didn't accomplish much at all. Even though the relief I got was miniscule, I was willing to take any relief I could get.

When I got back to the bed, they gave me juice to drink, to refill the well, I suppose. After all, the ultrasound works best on a full bladder.

Every fifteen or twenty minutes, I'd have to use the bathroom. It was ridiculous, really, but it was an urge I couldn't fight. I never had to go this often even when I was nine months along. I was frustrated, confused, and grumpy. Anytime they tried to talk me out of going, I became irritated. Every time I asked if the ultrasound people were here, they told me, "no, but they're on their way." The pain was intensifying, and I was angry at the whole hospital staff, at the whole world for that matter. I stopped listening to them and their "full bladder" mantra and just did what I needed to do.

"You know, you aren't being very nice to the nurses," Pam whispered as I sipped on a straw that jutted out of a cup of juice that someone had shoved into my hand.

Small wonder.

It added insult to injury that every time I plodded into the bathroom, my stomach looked bigger than the time before. On my first bathroom break, the mirror reflected back to me what could be mistaken for a four-month pregnancy, when in reality I was only about one month along. Over the course of several bathroom visits, even though it made no sense to me, my belly seemed to gradually grow to the size of a seven-month pregnancy.

Four hours from the time I was moved into the room to wait, the ultrasound machine and technician showed up. By then, I was hurting more than I could ever remember hurting in my entire life.

I was told to lie down again. The touch of the ultra sound device on my abdomen felt like pressing on a fresh bruise. Everything hurt. I wanted them to stop, but they ignored my moans and stared at the ultrasound monitor, concern carved into every one of their faces. "Take a picture of this," one would say. Then they'd move the device to the other side of my abdomen. "Take a picture of that."

I pulled out from my fog of pain long enough to ask, "Take a picture of what?"

"Just some fluid."

If I had been thinking clearly, I would have made an association with the lack of blood flow that would be expected during a miscarriage to the fairly rapid expansion of my abdomen. I was bleeding internally, and the doctors were taking pictures of the blood, but at that time I didn't feel good enough to summon the energy to question them further.

When blood travels in its normal channels of vessels and veins, it is a great thing to have, in fact, you can't live without it. But blood vessels have a protective coating inside that prevents blood enzymes from irritating them. When blood leaks out into places it isn't meant to be, and comes in contact with body parts that aren't built to withstand chemicals in the blood, the enzymes create irritation to the organs or other body parts it comes in contact with, triggering the body's natural immune system to fight the foreign material that's sight-seeing in places it's not allowed to go. The increasing amount of blood inside my abdomen was also the culprit that made me run to the bathroom so often, because it created pressure on my bladder that was not to be ignored as my abdominal cavity filled to near bursting with blood.

Immediate surgery was needed to stop the bleeding. After the doctors left to prepare for the procedure, the nurses had me change into one of those infamous little hospital gowns with the openings that manage to sneak open when you aren't looking. Then they loaded me into a wheelchair with just a strap of vinyl across the back to support my shoulders. I tried to arrange my hospital gown to cover up anything that shouldn't show, but since there were no rear view mirrors, I didn't know if I'd accomplished my goal.

While rolling toward the surgery room, we passed one of my doctors in the hall. "I hope no one can see my backside," I said.

The doctor laughed. Knowing that my pain relief was imminent, I was able to summon a smile in return.

Later, the doctor told me that he wouldn't have laughed if he'd known how serious the situation really was. But at the time it felt good to smile again, since no one knew what awaited us in the operating room.

As soon as I was wheeled into surgery, I looked around in surprise. I had always imagined a surgery room to be large and full of technical equipment, such as wires, monitors, and all kinds of beeping screens accompanied by the *shush, shush* of complex medical machinery.

To tell the truth, there just wasn't much in there. The central point was a steel table high enough for the doctors to stand around when they performed surgery. There wasn't any padding on it at all. I guess it was the best way to keep it sterile.

A nurse was checking over the surgery instruments on a stainless steel table that had wheels on each leg, and the anesthesiologist adjusted dials on a machine that was no bigger than a little refrigerator found in some motel rooms.

"Is this all?" I blurted out.

The anesthesiologist glanced up at me. "Yeah, this is it. There's not much to look at, is there?"

I stared at the surgery table with some trepidation. It was higher than the seat in my van, so there was no way I'd be able to climb up on that thing. Fortunately, someone thought to bring in the kind of hospital bed that rises up and down. They rolled it into place next to the surgery table.

Since it was in its lowest position, I was able to push myself out of the wheelchair and climb onto it. Once I was in place, the bed was raised to the height of the operating table. So far, so good. My ordeal was nearly ended.

Someone asked me to scoot over onto the surgery table. My brain told my body to comply, but it wouldn't. Frustrated, I tried to move again, but my body again refused to obey. Without any help from me, two people at my shoulders and two at my feet finally managed to help me scoot partway onto the table.

What was wrong with me? Was I paralyzed? A voice cut through my fear and frustration. For all I know, it was the nurse who thought I didn't have any right to scream when I wasn't actually having a baby.

"Can't you—" the voice said.

Then I was out of my body and looking down at myself from the far left corner of the room.

CHAPTER 5

Fighting Death

Time seemed to stand still for me, even though the doctors and nurses went about preparing for surgery. Not one of them so much as glanced at the body on the operating table. No one was even near it.

In spite of their oblivion to my new vantage point, I knew that it wasn't normal for me to be up that high. I hadn't even had any anesthesia yet.

My mind was suddenly filled with details of the story my mother-in-law, Judy, had told me soon after I married into the Freeman family. Her second child, Jesse, had to be delivered C-section. When she woke up from the anesthesia, she was hit with a truckload of pain, and began screaming. The next thing she knew, she was at the top of the room looking down on a woman screaming and screaming, writhing in agony on a bed.

Someone please help that woman, she thought. *That lady needs help. Oh, I hope someone can help her soon.*

A man sat on a chair next to the woman's bed. He leaned over and whispered, "Stop that, you're embarrassing me."

Judy was instantly back inside her body, staring up at the face of her husband, Bill. "How dare you tell me not to scream!" she yelled. "You don't know how I feel!"

Then she stopped, realizing that she had been outside of her body, looking down on it. As amazed as she was by realizing that she had left her body, she was equally surprised that she hadn't recognized herself.

There are some accounts I've heard of people dying who have no clue that they've crossed the invisible line of mortality until a heavenly messenger comes to greet them, or until they begin traveling through a long tunnel toward a light. Maybe this is because people generally tend to think that they'll live forever. Since we can't really imagine what death is like, we figure that it could never happen to us, at least not in the near future. Maybe we're so comfortable with our life that we don't want to think of the life that comes after this one.

Perhaps it was because I'd heard my mother-in-law's story, but when I found myself up against the ceiling looking down at the woman on the surgery table, I knew in an instant that body was mine. It also meant something else: I was dead.

No way, I thought. I wasn't going anywhere. I could still see my body, and I was going back. For years, I'd pushed a premonition that I was going to die at a young age way back into my subconscious, and now I fought it with every particle of my being. I refused to leave mortality before my children were raised. I was going back into my body no matter what.

It was like hearing about people who survive a ride over a waterfall in a barrel, then suddenly finding myself plopped in a barrel at the edge of the falls. Well, I intended to scramble out of that barrel as fast as possible. My children still needed me. My oldest was only fourteen, for goodness sake, and my youngest was not yet two. The thought of them trying to get along without a mother to cook their meals, wash their clothes, settle their squabbles, smooth bandages over their scrapes, and kiss away their pain was unthinkable. In my mind, it simply wasn't an option.

I know that mothers of small children sometimes die. I know that there are children who are orphaned from both parents while still young. Life's situations are as varied as there are people on earth. I cannot speak for anyone else, and I cannot claim to know anyone else's mission or purpose for this life, but I wasn't ready to leave yet.

For myself, I believe that everyone's past affects them to some extent, even when they become adults.

I've heard a lot of people blame their childhoods for their situations and say that they can't help the way they are now because of how they were raised or what happened to them as children, but I believe that people reach a point where they make their own choices, no matter what their past has been.

A lot of people have grown up without their mothers and have turned out just fine. Then there are others, like me, who have grown up with mothers who weren't able to function in a normal nurturing capacity. Being emotionally unavailable stems from reasons as varied in number as the spectrum colors of a rainbow.

In my case, my mother had a mental illness that has not been definitively diagnosed, but whatever it is, our family suffered through more than one of her nervous breakdowns. One doctor diagnosed her with too much stress and gave her bi-polar medication. One offered the possibility of schizophrenia. All I know is, she was on prescriptions for Lithium and Thorazine. When she was on her medication, she was pretty much tranquilized and slept a lot, making her uninvolved in our lives. We were left to our own devices. My mother is a very good person, but she was emotionally detached. She didn't yell at us—she was just oblivious. If something got hard, she never wanted to deal with it. No matter what the cause, mental illness is hard to understand, especially for a child.

One notable facet of my childhood playtime is that I never did like playing with Barbies. They weren't the least bit huggable, not even when they were dressed in all their furs. I was drawn to baby dolls, and spent my playtime changing them, feeding them, and singing lullabies while I rocked them and held them close. Perhaps I was subconsciously filling a gap that I felt from my own early years.

Whatever the reason, I'm not complaining. I'm only giving this insight to explain why my heart was set on staying with my children. I simply could not stand the thought of them growing up without their mother. Since no one had been able to fill the role of my emotionally absent mother in my developmental years, I couldn't see how anyone could do that for my children. I simply love being a mom, and the need to be available for my children is an innate part of me. Everyone on the earth has challenges, and working to overcome the lack of a mother's adequate involvement in my young life is mine. I just felt within my heart that no one could love, nurture, or understand my children as well as I did.

As much as I love James and appreciate him providing for our family, how can an on-the-road trucker possibly take care of household chores along with a house full of children? I couldn't imagine any other solution for him, should he find himself a widower, except to split up the children between relatives, who are big-hearted and generous, but who have large families of their own. I couldn't think of one single person who could take on all seven children and keep them together.

Yet my children needed to stay together in the framework of our own family, and I needed to be the one to take care of them, no matter how many dirty diapers, runny noses, forever hungry mouths and mountains of laundry they created. No matter that I didn't seem to have more than a minute to myself every day, and that was in the bathroom. (After one minute, there would come the inevitable pounding on the door and cries of "Mommy! Mommy!") I couldn't bear the thought of my little ones deprived of the nurturing that had been painfully lacking in my own childhood. I simply wasn't going to leave my children without their mother. I love every aspect of mothering, and I wasn't done yet. I was staying.

Since my decision was made, I didn't bother looking around. I didn't even consider that there might be a choice to stay or go. My mind was anchored in the mortal realm, my eyes fixed on my earthly remains, and I headed back toward my body like a kamikaze pilot.

Someone grabbed me, and I stopped as suddenly as if I'd hit a glass wall. I whirled around and stared at a large hand that gripped my upper arm, a strong, perfect hand marred by a cruel puncture wound in the very center. My eyes flew up to stare into a familiar face. The blue eyes lit up with love and delight when my glance met his. The smooth cheeks above his chestnut beard lifted into a warm smile. It was Jesus Christ who had hold of me, and with a voice full of love he said, "Come with me."

Even though his gentle words washed over me in a wave of peace, I panicked. In the few times I'd contemplated my own death, I had thought that my grandma or grandpa would come to get me. I never, ever imagined that I would merit being escorted by Christ himself, who had to be far too busy to come for the likes of me. I'm just a mother and a housewife, not anyone important like a prophet or a patriarch. Why would he come to escort insignificant me?

While a part of me was drawn to Christ, knowing it would be heavenly to abandon my bloated and bruised body to go with him, another part of me recoiled. *Uh, oh, I'm a goner. If Christ has come for me personally, then my number is up for sure. What will happen to my children? They still need me. I have to go back.*

I'm afraid that part of my desire to stay was selfish, because I find great personal joy in raising my children. From the time I was a teenager, my fondest career goal was to get married and have babies. I did a lot of babysitting, which I would have been happy to do for free. After a few basic Home Economic classes, I further taught myself by trial and error to become an accomplished cook. My mother helped with my school sewing projects, but after I was grown, she confessed that she thought I'd never learn the skill. She said it was frustrating to work with me because it took so long for me to catch on. I'm glad I didn't know that then, because I persevered and enjoy sewing to this day. All of these experiences readied me for my chosen career of becoming a mother.

When James and I had our first daughter, it was like bringing a piece of heaven to earth. I never considered the time I spent caring for her as work. I once spoke to a lady who complained about how much work her baby was. I was startled. How could that be? I loved the job of being a mom more than anything.

With my thoughts firmly fastened on the upcoming plight of my motherless children, I wasn't even close to a rational frame of mind. All I knew was that I had to get back to my body so that I could take care of my children.

"I have to go back," I said as I tried to pull away from Christ's grasp. I twisted and squirmed and kicked, stretching my free arm toward my body on the operating table. I thought of each one of my children, and their individual personalities. How could I possibly help them grow up to their full potential from the spirit world? Thinking of them gave me fresh impetus to fight against the hand that held me. I didn't want to look at Christ's face again, afraid that it might weaken my resolve. If only I could get back into my body before he spoke again, with a voice that penetrated through my very soul, then it would be easier for me to carry through my desperate desire. I struggled like a fish held by the tail, hovering over an expanse of life-giving water. My efforts to escape were as fierce as a grizzly bear breaking free to protect her cub. I was so desperate to get back that I didn't even consider the matter open for discussion. I gave a final reckless lunge and nearly broke free.

"Whoa," Christ said. He anchored his other hand around my waist. I could sense his frustration, and felt more than heard the words, *For most people, that's all it takes, just, "Come with me."*

It was foolish to think that I could get away from the Lord, but I wasn't thinking in the eternal realm. I was thinking of all those little flesh and blood bodies currently in the care of my sister Ruth Ann.

If I'd just taken the time to listen instead of throwing a fit like a two-year-old being told "no" in a candy store, then Christ would have had a chance to explain.

"There are people who want to see you," he said.

"Then you'll have to bring them to me, because I'm not going."

CHAPTER 6
Just Visiting

Jesus laughed. In that very instant, I stopped struggling, mesmerized by the incredibly joyous sound that came out of his mouth—a perfect, beautiful blend of happiness, light and love. This absolutely amazing sound pierced my spirit and filled every corner of my being with warmth and delight. The Savior's laugh was infinitely calming and reassuring, boosting my spirit and working the miracle of making any worries insignificant. There are no earthly words to describe it, but in the moment I heard Jesus' marvelous laugh, my heart soared, and I was filled with delight and a sense of utter safety and peace. If a laugh could ever be described as handsome, that was it.

I've heard that humor can make a difference in helping people heal more quickly from disease, and after hearing the remarkable sound of the Lord's laughter, I am totally convinced of its power.

Wow, I thought. *The Lord laughed!* I always liked to

believe that he had a sense of humor, but I still had an image stuck in my head that he would present himself as more serious and dignified. I had a lot to learn.

Embarrassed by the tantrum I'd just thrown, I gave Jesus a small smile, feeling foolish for fighting against his touch just moments earlier. I needed to make him understand why I had done it. Forgetting for the moment that he knew me better than I even know myself, I said, "I can't leave my children."

Still chuckling, the sound like a warm waterfall flowing over me in soft waves, Jesus answered, "I promise, you can come back."

I should have known that with his great love and infinite kindness, the Lord would let me choose to return. I could have saved myself a lot of awkwardness if I had just talked to him before I'd decided to take matters into my own hands.

I still didn't want to leave my body alone down there without me in it.

"How long will I be gone?" I asked.

Christ glanced down at the activity below us. "In mortality, it will only be a few moments. Time is not the same where we're going."

When I looked down at myself lying pale and still on the surgery table, time seemed to stand still. As I hesitated with my answer, I could feel Christ's love wrapped around me, an amazing presence that was so powerful it penetrated right through me. As if it touched a trigger somewhere in my heart, I realized that the Lord wouldn't make a promise he couldn't keep. I turned to him with a grin and said, "Okay. I'll go."

Christ smiled, his face alight with joy and love as he took my hand.

I know that some people say they go through tunnels when they die, moving toward a light at the end of it. For me, it wasn't that way. Perhaps that would have seemed too final, or too confining with no way to turn around and go back. Or perhaps since the Lord is the light that most people move toward, and since he was standing right next to me, there was no need to go through a tunnel.

We turned away from the operating room and faced a long flight of perfectly white stairs. There were no seams anywhere to be seen. The steps were faultless, and made of a hard substance with a matte finish, like one solid piece of marble. The staircase was about twenty feet wide. We started climbing, and we went up several flights of stairs, which had occasional landings in between them. I climbed the stairs with ease. I was pleased to discover that my spirit body was slender and energetic. I had left all my "baby fat" lying on the surgery table with my earthly body, and I didn't miss it a bit. After all those steps I wasn't even tired.

"You showed perfect love," Jesus said.

"What?" I turned to gaze up at him. He is quite a bit taller than me, well over six feet, maybe even pushing seven feet tall. I stand about 5' 6", and my head barely reached his chest.

"You wanted to stay with your children instead of coming with me," he said in a voice that wasn't the least bit offended.

As soon as I wondered about his lack of hurt feelings at my refusal to accompany him without a fight, the thought came to me that Jesus is my Savior, that he gave his life in order to guarantee my free agency, just as he has guaranteed the agency of everyone on the earth. Every living person has the freedom to choose what they do from day to day. However, if they choose to break the laws or partake of any addictive substance or habit, they are not free to choose the consequence. It will follow their actions and usually reduce the range of choices they can make for their future. For example, if someone were to choose to commit a crime, they could be sentenced to jail and not have the freedom to go where they wanted to. If someone chose to drink, they could become an alcoholic and be limited in the choices they have in how their body will function.

I had the freedom to choose to fight against going anywhere I didn't want to go or doing anything I didn't want to do, and Christ did not condemn me for it. I realized that Jesus came personally for me because if he'd sent one of my relatives, they may not have been able to overcome my determination to immediately return to my body. He was the only one who had the power to convince me to go to the spirit world. He knew I would put up a fight and dig in my heels, so in his wisdom, he came to get me himself.

I heard a heavenly choir with herald angels burst into glorious song, every note pitched to absolute perfection. I lifted my eyes toward the top of the stairs, trying to locate the source of the incredible voices that blended and harmonized and soared in a breathtaking melody.

As I wondered at the magnificent voices, the realization came to my mind that anyone who wants to can sing in the heavenly choir. There are no try-outs, and there are no eliminations. If you want to sing, you're in.

When my mind focused on the words they were singing, I was astonished to discover their song was about me. They sang about my desire to stay with my children in order to raise them. I have no idea how they came up with the words and music in such a short time, but it was a song of praise and joy, and it had my name in it, sort of like songs people write to commemorate good deeds on earth, like *The Ballad of Davy Crockett* or *The Star Spangled Banner.* I was truly humbled.

I need to emphasize that this experience was geared for me, my individual spirit and my own personal calling. Everyone is different, everyone's situation is unique, and sometimes people are needed more in heaven than on earth.

Regardless of what each individual's calling is, the heavenly choir loves to sing of great and wonderful things that are done both in heaven and on earth. There is always music in heaven and something to sing about.

Before I could locate the choir, I noticed gates at the top of the stairs. The closed gates were at least fifteen feet tall and made of gleaming gold bars twisted together into an intricate design. They were flawlessly crafted and beautiful to look upon. As we drew closer, I could make out the silhouette of a man's head in the exact center of each gate, a perfect profile outlined in gold and set sideways, like an old-fashioned cameo. Each profile was surrounded by an oval of shining gold beads that gleamed with perfect symmetry and beauty. When we reached the gates, I recognized the profile as that of Jesus Christ.

Of course, I thought. *Christ is the gatekeeper.*

Delicate gold bars twisted their way down either side of the matched profiles in a gorgeous pattern that would be difficult to replicate on earth, although the old-fashioned wrought iron Victorian-era gates are the closest comparison I can think of. The gates were hinged to heavy gold pillars on either side. Beyond the pillars stretched a golden fence with bars of gold twisted and curled and fashioned into intricate designs that were absolutely beautiful.

I was amazed to see that heaven was fenced off. I had heard references to "The Pearly Gates" several times in my life, but I always thought it was just a figure of speech. Yet standing in front of the faultless workmanship before me, I figured that whoever had come up with that description must not have made a personal visit, since the gates I saw were made of gleaming gold, so stunning that I could never imagine getting tired of looking at them.

The gates swung inward, and a cheer went up from the throng of people who watched us enter. I was somewhat confused by all the commotion. I glanced around at the cheering faces before my eyes focused on some familiar and much-loved features, and I stopped in my tracks.

"Grandma!" I called. I moved through the joyful throng toward my Grandma Burton. Some people were actually jumping up and down like cheerleaders heading up a winning cheer. I grabbed Grandma in a long embrace, and the people all around us burst into applause, laughing and calling "Hooray!" Even though Grandma looked younger than she had on earth, I still recognized her. I was sixteen years old when she died.

"Hello, Suzie," she said, returning my affectionate squeeze. "It's so good to see you again." The seventeen years that we'd been apart fell away, and it was as if she'd always been there for me.

A man's voice interrupted our little reunion. "Well, Suz, you acted just like that as a kid, too."

I let go of Grandma and whirled around to see another beloved face grinning at me. "Grandpa Scholes!" I cried, and moved into his arms. After a moment I pulled away and asked him, "I acted just like what?"

"Stubborn," he said, with a twinkle in his eye. "We could never make you go anywhere you didn't want to go. Sometimes we had to pick you up and carry you, kicking and screaming, until we were all bruised and deaf."

I laughed in delight. It had been eleven years since Grandpa had passed over, and it was good to hear his banter again.

Communication in heaven is different. We spoke mind to mind, using just our thoughts. Since understanding is perfect, there is no confusion as to what someone means. The feeling pours out along with the words, so there is no misunderstanding whatsoever. This is perfect communication, and the best part of all is that only love is spoken here.

James' sister, Connie Sue, moved in to hug me. I recognized her at once, even though I'd only seen photographs, because she'd been dragged to death by a horse when she was only fifteen. James was eleven at the time, yet carried such fond memories of his older sister that we named one of our daughters Connie Suzanne.

Now I was actually in the arms of my daughter's namesake. "Connie!" I said as I returned her embrace.

"Good to see you," Connie said, and pulled away to give me a warm smile. I had sometimes wondered at the way Connie had died, whether it hadn't been a tragic accident that could have been avoided so that she could grow up, marry, and bring children to earth. But gazing into her beautiful, calm eyes, I felt an assurance that it had been her time to pass on to the next life. It was no accident that she was here.

I gave Connie's hands an affectionate squeeze. "It's good to see you, too."

There were a few others from my family that I recognized from sharing our time on earth. James' Grandma Freeman was there, and I greeted her with as much joy as my own relatives. She is such a neat lady, and I love her so much. It had cast a pall over both Christmas Eve's that had come and gone since she passed away on December 24, 1996.

"Stop feeling sad for me," she whispered in my ear

as she gave me a hug. "Have joyous Christmas Eves, Suzie, it's a wonderful time. Be happy because I am happy. Okay?"

"Okay," I agreed as I felt Grandma's joy encompass me.

Most of the family who greeted me had come and gone before I was born, yet even if I hadn't seen their photographs, I knew they were my family. The ties were not quite as tight as the ones I had with those who had shared part of my earthly experience, but no matter how well I knew them, I was pleased to see and acknowledge them all.

We mingled in a beautiful garden, with perfectly smooth walkways that appeared to be made from the same seamless material as the steps. The walks were lined with flowers that were mesmerizing in their perfection. My grandparents helped run the American Fork Nursery, and my dad owned and operated a wholesale nursery and landscaping business, so I was familiar with plants and intrigued with these gorgeous flowers.

When I bent to take a closer look, I was astonished that I could actually see the flowers moving to the music of the choir. Then I realized that not only were they swaying in perfect time to the voices singing in precise harmony, they were also making flawless music of their own, like an orchestra accompanying the vocals. I couldn't imagine how they were doing it. There was no place I could see that they could hide a tiny violin or bassoon, but they were making faultless music just the same.

They appeared to be a type of orchid or lily, and no two flowers were the same. Their coloring was absolutely exquisite. It was as though a master painter had strolled down the path and stopped to paint each one individually. Some had pretty colored tips, some had delicate stripes of one, two, or three different shades, and some were all one color. The petals were glass-like, each one glowing and reflecting light in a way that was subtle, yet undeniable. There really aren't any words to describe it. The best thing I can think of in earthly terms is that they had a light within them that made them shine with a soft glow, sort of like tin foil, only without the metallic gleam. They were absolutely beautiful.

The grass was also perfect, with every single blade the same height, and each piece of grass a brilliant green. People wearing white robes sat on the grass, talking to one another. The lawn was softer than the most luxurious carpet, even carpet that had the benefit of double padding. The deep azure blue sky was cloudless. Even though there was light everywhere, I couldn't tell where it was coming from. There was no obvious source, like a sun.

Christ put his arm around my shoulders in a brotherly hug filled with love, then led me down a white pathway that curved like a stream meandering through lush country meadows.

Along both sides of the path were a few trees, round and not too tall, that resembled globe willows. No two were exactly alike, and not very many bore fruit. One tree had white fruit about the size and shape of a pear, but it was covered all over with bumps. It was very juicy, and glowed with a bright white inner light. I knew it was a sacred fruit, but didn't know why.

There was also a light-green star fruit. It had a pod with five sections that radiated from a connected center. When cut, the slices resemble stars.

There was one unusual fruit in the shape of vivid red stars hanging from the branches of another tree.

It was made known to me that there were also "Trees of Life" growing in various places throughout the garden, their branches spreading out a comforting canopy of cool blue shade that invited any weary spirits to come and rest. Anyone who spends time in the shade of these trees is infused with new energy and strength drawn from the special properties of the tree. When the spirits again feel refreshed, they walk away, leaving their fatigue behind.

Some may wonder, as I did, why spirits would ever get tired. It seems to us on earth that only our mortal bodies would get worn out and need to rest. The answer I received is that our spirits can get weary, too.

Take, for example, a day that you might spend studying a certain subject or pouring a lot of concentration into a project that doesn't require any physical exertion, but takes a lot of brain power. You don't spend this time running up and down hills or putting out any notable physical exertion, yet when the day is spent, you may feel just as fatigued as if you'd run a marathon. You've depleted your mental, emotional, or spiritual energy, and you feel as if you need a rest before going back to your course of study again.

It was also made known to me that guardian angels often rest beneath these trees in order to gain strength after going through a difficult time with their charges on earth.

CHAPTER 7

Amphitheater

I soon noticed someone hurrying toward us. The LDS prophet Joseph Smith was all but running along the path, his arm outstretched for a handshake and a beautiful grin spread across his face. In his deep voice, he said, "I have to shake the hand of the lady who actually told Christ 'no.'"

I was taken aback. When I wondered what he meant, it came to my mind that sometimes it's okay to say "no," because you have your agency. That's the whole reason Christ died for us. People have the right to choose for themselves what they do, and that's why the Lord wasn't going to make me go with him when he met me on the ceiling of the operating room. I had to agree to go.

He is pleased when we use our agency, he wants us to make choices that we think are best for us, and he hopes that we use our agency for our best good. If someone happens to choose amiss, they always have the option of repenting or else suffering the natural consequences of their choice.

Right behind Joseph Smith was the prophet Brigham Young. He waited his turn to greet me with a look of patient tolerance as Joseph Smith pumped my arm up and down.

Brigham Young shook my hand in a more constrained fashion. "I'm so very honored to meet you," he said, tipping his top hat.

His words took me by surprise. He had it altogether backwards, because it was my privilege and good fortune to meet *him*.

Joseph Smith and Brigham Young both appeared to be about six feet tall, but that included Brigham Young with his top hat on. Their clothes were of the same style that they would have worn while living in their time period on earth. I wondered about this, and it was made known to me that they could have chosen to wear anything they wanted to. It was for my benefit in recognizing them that they chose to dress the way they did.

Then, without any warning and to my great surprise, Joseph Smith took a running leap onto the grass beside us and performed a perfect double back flip. I stood there with my mouth open, my eyes wide in amazement. I'd heard stories about how athletic he was and how he liked to play games, but I never expected to see anything like that. I thought that heaven would be more serious, with everyone going about in solemn fervor, doing God's work. I had never imagined that there would be cheering and laughing and double back flips.

I came to understand that if there is a celebration to have, they have it. If someone is very happy, they can show it any way they please. Heavenly beings are not bound by gravity, and there is no pride or self-consciousness. You don't worry what someone else is thinking about you, because everyone there has pure love for one another. Joseph was expressing his joy over meeting me, and celebrating how happy he was with my desire to stay and care for my children above the chance to enjoy a life free from bodily ills in heaven. I was truly astonished that he seemed so tickled to meet me that he could scarcely contain himself. I thought it should be the other way around, because I was surely excited to meet him, but I didn't dare try a back flip, even without the handicap of my earthly body. I thought he was overreacting a bit, as I had only done what any mother would do.

"Joseph, now is not the time," Brigham Young said.

"I don't care," Joseph replied with a grin.

I realized that Joseph Smith freely shows his emotions, as he did in his earthly life. We will all take our dominant personality traits with us when we pass on to the other side, for good or ill. If we are diligent on earth, we will be diligent in heaven. If we carry around a habit of complaining or finding fault, we will be that way when we pass over. If we like to crack jokes, we'll likely be cracking jokes for eternity.

Before I died, I thought that when people went to the other side of the veil that they would instantly know and remember everything from the time before they were born. In reality, memories of our pre-mortal life do not come back all of a sudden. It takes time to remember the things of heaven.

It's kind of like taking a long boat trip across the ocean. At first you might have to hold on to the railing in order to keep from stumbling. You have to hang on or put your arms out for balance until you get used to the unaccustomed motion. When you become adapted to the back and forth and up and down movement of the sea, you are said to have your "sea legs," and walking around the boat is as comfortable and familiar as your own name.

Later, when the boat is docked and you get off on solid ground, the land seems to be moving under your feet. Even though you know that you walked on land before your boat trip, it still takes time to remember how to balance and maneuver around on firm ground. You have to hold onto a railing to keep from falling until you get your land legs back.

That is what it's like when we pass away. It takes awhile to absorb what has happened and to begin thinking in a spiritual way,

Now that I look back and understand how free my spirit was, I wish I'd gone ahead and tried a back flip of my own!

Joseph Smith and Brigham Young had their families with them. I remember Emma Smith and Marianne Young dressed in clothes appropriate to their era on earth. They were clapping and cheering as I greeted the former prophets. It was great fun for me to meet those wonderful women, too. They have so much beauty and radiate love and goodwill to others. They were very much like this while they were on earth, too. Through meeting them, I came to realize that the old saying, "Behind every great man is a great woman," is true. Joseph's parents and brothers and sisters were there, as well as several others. It was quite a celebration.

Many other people began crowding in behind the prophets and their wives, lining up to shake my hand. Most of them wore white robes with different pastel-colored sashes knotted around their waists, the ends falling free. Each color denoted a different calling for each individual. The men's robes were designed to hit them at mid-calf with sleeves ending just below their elbows. The women's robes were of a slightly different style, long enough to touch their ankles with sleeves that reached down to their wrists. It was only then that I realized I was wearing a white dress tied with a white sash.

I turned to look up at Christ, thinking that all these people wanted to see him for some reason. He returned my gaze, and in the depths of his eyes I saw that he could read my thoughts and knew of my confusion.

"They are celebrating the love you show for your children," he said to me with his thoughts.

"But I really didn't do anything out of the ordinary," I protested.

Christ raised his eyebrows and gave me a smile. "Little sister, don't you know how pleased I am with you?" He swept his hand around the gathering crowd. "We are all proud of you, but I think this might be easier if I take you to the amphitheater."

In a moment, we were standing in the center of a huge amphitheater built in a style that reminded me of the ancient Greeks, where rows of seats go up and up and up all the way around the arena. This amphitheater had no fence or barricade of any kind to keep the spectators off the arena floor. There were thousands and thousands of seats surrounding us, maybe even half a million, terraced up and around us on all sides. I was amazed to see that all the seats were full of people ready to listen to Christ's words. I felt sure that they had really come to see Christ, not me.

"Good deeds do not go unnoticed," Christ said with a reassuring smile. I wondered if I'd ever get used to him reading my mind.

Ironically, I never had liked being singled out for special notice, even as a child. When I was a little girl, people would often comment on the dimples in my cheeks. Whenever any grown ups (kids never mentioned them) said something to me about my cute dimples, I would immediately stop smiling, clamp my mouth shut, and tighten my facial muscles in an effort to hide them. Without exception, the grown ups would laugh, which frustrated me further since I was making such a huge effort to pinch my mouth in tight enough that they would never see me smile. Little did I know that when I clamped my mouth together and pulled in my cheeks, the dimples showed up even more!

My family was still with me in the amphitheater. Indeed, they accompanied me throughout all of my heavenly travels, offering quiet and loving background support.

With Jesus beside me I wasn't afraid to face all those heavenly beings. There is never fear when Christ is with you. There is actually no fear in heaven at all, only love.

The depth of Christ's love took me by surprise. It is as real and pervasive as a hearty bowl of hot soup when you come in after spending the whole day out in below zero weather. It reaches out and warms you through and through, nourishing you and making you feel secure and comforted. Christ would frequently rest his hand on my shoulder or encircle me with his powerful arm, his gentle touch actual proof that he did, indeed, take a personal interest in me and my welfare. Whenever he was close to me he would touch me. There are no words to express how much love Christ has for each one of us.

In spite of his presence, I felt inadequate standing in front of those thousands of people who wanted to see me. I realized in a single shrinking moment that not only does it take time to remember our previous spiritual lives after we die, it also takes time to overcome a poor self-image. I'd dragged my low self-esteem right with me through the veil, and it was sticking to me like an unwanted cocklebur.

Jesus addressed the crowd, explaining that I had shown perfect love for my children. Everyone already knew what I had done, as plainly as if they'd watched it on a big screen, but he went over the main points again. While describing my struggle to get away from him, a ripple of laughter swept the theater, but it was friendly laughter from people who cared about me, and I didn't feel ashamed.

"Most people fight against the idea of returning from heaven to earth to finish their work," Christ said.

"Only after they see the importance of their missions do they agree to return to mortality and finish what they covenanted to do."

As soon as Christ said that, I realized that my life hadn't flashed before my eyes. Since I'd heard that happens when people die, I wondered why it hadn't happened to me. The answer came that since I had already determined that I wasn't going to stay, there was no need to show my life in review yet. There also wasn't a need to show me what would happen if I had chosen to stay or to go back, since my mind was already made up and Christ had given me his promise that I could return.

Christ continued to address the crowd. He said, "Then there are those who are sufficiently finished with their missions on earth that they can choose to stay in heaven or go back. Almost all of them stay, and we're glad to have every one of them." Another chuckle rose from the assembly. "You know there is always choice, even in the missions undertaken by those in the mortal realm, and everyone is given their agency even when they pass back through the veil."

I felt that Christ was explaining this more for my benefit than of those assembled, but no one seemed to mind hearing it all again. "Instead of insisting on staying in heaven with us, Suzie insisted that she didn't even want to come in and look around. All of her thoughts were focused on the welfare of her children."

Christ gazed at me as though I'd just drawn an award-winning picture, and he was eager to show it off to everyone.

Have you ever heard the saying, "If God had a refrigerator, your picture would be on it?" That's just how it felt. Christ is proud and happy for everyone who accomplishes good things, and today was my day to be his "Show and Tell." People in heaven love to see good deeds of any sort. They give glory to those who do good, and whenever good things happen on earth, they cheer.

Even though Christ's arm around me kept me feeling secure, I still didn't believe that I deserved all the recognition I was getting. My decision to stay on earth hadn't been difficult. I just wanted to mother my children, as simple as that.

CHAPTER 8

Garden of Eden

When we finished at the amphitheater, Christ led me along a path that wound its way into a stand of lush foliage, the thickest I'd ever seen. Leaves of various shades of green were so brilliantly colored that it almost hurt to look at them. It was so thick that I couldn't see any place to step off the trail, even along the sections that had no trees. Brilliant, colorful flowers burst out from between the glossy green leaves, nodding to us as we strolled past. In places, trees and vines made walls for us to walk between, and I was amazed at the beautiful variety that surrounded us.

We soon came upon a clearing where a man and a woman dressed in white stood before a charming, old-world cottage, watching us approach with eager anticipation. When we drew closer, I was amazed to see that they both stood at least seven feet tall. I knew them in an instant. They were my ancestors, Adam and Eve, the very first people placed on earth.

Even though Eve was as tall as a professional basketball player, she was perfectly proportioned and moved without a hint of the awkwardness that sometimes plagues extremely tall people who can't keep up with their long limbs. Her every movement was done with ease and grace, and it was apparent that Eve was meant to be tall. Her white robe was belted around the slender waist of her lovely figure. Long blonde hair glimmered and shifted against her white gown when she moved to hug me.

Adam's hair was cut short and was darker than Eve's, as though it had been blonde when he was a boy but had darkened with age.

"What an honor to meet you," Eve said, pulling away from our embrace.

What? She's honored to meet me? My poor self-esteem tried to reassert itself.

Eve invited me into her quaint home. It reminded me of the house the seven dwarves lived in on Disney's animated movie, *Snow White*, but it was much larger, of course. It was decorated all in earth tones, and everything in it looked like it was handmade of natural materials such as wood and stone by an expert craftsman. Their dining table was huge, with benches running down each side and a big chair on either end. Fresh picked flowers set inside a clay pitcher brightened up the center of the table, which was large enough to seat twenty people. I found myself wondering where I could get a table that size! On the hearth next to a large fireplace stood a round black metal pot. A lovely woven willow chair that appeared comfortable and inviting sat in one corner of the fireplace room, with books resting on a small wooden table to one side of it.

Adam and Eve loved simplicity, and only kept around them the things that they needed. I didn't see a single thing in their home that was out of place or that I would describe as intricate or fussy.

When I was done walking through their home, Adam grinned with anticipation. As eager as a child ready to show me his favorite plaything, he took hold of my arm and hurried me outside to show me around the spirit world version of the Garden of Eden. Speaking with great fervor and laughing often, he told me about how he and Eve had loved their time in the Garden so much on earth that they re-created it in heaven. Adam has a refreshing and vibrant zest for life, and I enjoyed the way he treated me like a favorite little sister.

He pointed up into the canopy of leaves and branches over our heads. I looked up and saw toucans, parrots, and brightly feathered birds that I didn't even know the names of. Monkeys swung through the trees, chattering with delight as soon as they spied Adam. There were several kinds of animals in the garden, some I'd never seen before.

Adam talked on and on, telling me about all the animals we saw and how he named them. When he pointed out the various plants and flowers, they captured my interest even more than the animals. I recognized some of the plants from working in my dad's greenhouses while growing up. It was obvious that Adam loved his garden. He had the original green thumb. He is an amazing man and a terrific big brother, and I enjoyed every moment of time I spent with him.

Just as we turned to head back toward the house, I was amazed to see a lion push its way out of the undergrowth, as easy and comfortable as a cat strolling across his own yard. My eyes widened in surprise, but I didn't feel any fear at having this king of beasts with his thick, golden mane walk past within easy biting distance of my leg.

I stuck my hand out as the lion padded by. He moved underneath my palm, totally unconcerned with my presence, as tame as a family dog. Not even breaking stride, he glided on beyond us and disappeared into the undergrowth.

Adam turned toward me, his eyes alight with glee. "Don't you just love it here?"

I admitted that I most certainly did.

Satisfied with my answer, Adam said, "Let's go find Eve, shall we?"

We came upon her in a clearing, where she sat on a wooden bench with her beautiful face tilted up toward the trees. When she heard us approach, she glanced at us and smiled in welcome. I sat on a bench opposite her. She leaned forward and took both of my hands in hers. Her skin was so soft and white that I was afraid my dishpan hands would suffer by comparison, but I didn't want to pull away.

It was easy to see why Eve had been chosen to be the mother of the whole human race. She and Adam were a perfect blend of personalities. I had imagined that Adam and Eve would be more king and queen-like instead of acting like an older brother and sister who wanted me to be happy and comfortable. I was aware of their important station, and I knew they had specific responsibilities, yet they didn't see themselves as better nor act is if they were more important than me or anyone else. They certainly didn't expect a curtsy or a salute or anything like that. They were accommodating, and easy to talk to. Both of them were family oriented, and came across as caring deeply for each other as well as the whole human race.

"I love being a mother, too," Eve said.

"You heard?" I asked, not remembering seeing Adam or Eve in the amphitheater or at heaven's gates.

"We sure did," Adam boomed in his hearty voice. "You're every bit as stubborn as a bear."

Eve laughed, her voice like the music of clear water running over smooth rocks. "Coming from him, that's a compliment," she assured me. "You know how mother bears are known for their ferocity in protecting their cubs? You were the same way."

"You, too," I countered, unwilling to bask in a spotlight I didn't feel like I deserved.

"We all do the best we know how."

I looked into Eve's clear green eyes and said, "May I ask you something?"

Eve's eyes sparkled and she blessed me with a perfect smile. "Yes, but I already know what you're going to say."

"Well, then?"

"I did have twins, several sets of them, in fact."

I felt an instant kinship with Eve and said, "I do love having babies, even twins, but I especially like having them when they come one at a time."

"Twins aren't so bad," Eve answered.

I smiled and nodded with knowing. "But sometimes I had to nurse them both at the same time."

Eve's eyebrows went up. "Me too, but it gets trickier with triplets. They have to learn that they'll get something to eat eventually. Then, when they get old enough to get around, they're always into things." She laughed again, and I joined in.

"I have to keep reminding myself that the housework will be there later, but my babies won't," I said. "I was 18 when I had my first baby, and I never even thought they were work until I had the twins. I'm just grateful I didn't have a third one."

"That's a good thing to be grateful for, but you would have handled it," Eve answered.

I thought of my twin pre-schoolers at home. The thought gave my heart a little twist as I imagined them growing up without their mother. But that wasn't going to happen, because Christ had promised to take me back.

CHAPTER 9

Heavenly Cities

Christ then took me to a massive palace set amidst sculptured gardens that were so perfect, they could have been plastic. No, they were too perfect to be plastic. Rather than the natural growth of the spiritual Garden of Eden we had just left, these shrubs were trimmed with exact edges, and the flowers were set in orderly rows, with some of the flowerbeds radiating colorful blooms out from a center point in planned precision.

We came to a set of massive doors, twelve feet high and appearing to be made of solid gold. I expected them to be terribly heavy, but Christ pulled them open without any trouble. A floor of flawless marble spread out before us from the golden threshold. The broad marble expanse swept into the palace interior, interrupted only by two massive marble pillars. The walls hung with thick, gold-embroidered draperies that warmed the room and muffled any echoes of sound.

Between the two pillars I could see an extraordinary man seated on a golden throne against the far wall. As we got closer, I saw that the back of the throne reached a height of about ten feet off the floor. A short flight of stairs led up to the throne's seat. It was hard for me to choose what to stare at first—the red-haired man in the shining golden crown, or the throne set with a dazzling array of jewels.

My eyes were drawn to the throne, where brilliant white pearls larger than I had ever imagined sat in delicate cages of gold, confining enough to keep the precious pearls secure, yet letting their iridescent faces shine through. Huge polished diamonds winked at me from their places among the golden scrollwork, and emeralds as large as my palm trimmed the throne with green, as dark and beautiful as the ocean is deep. I'd never seen such a dazzling piece of furniture. It pleased the eye and gladdened the heart just to look at it.

As I stared in amazement at the rich splendor, it was made known to me that we get in heaven what we earned on earth. The saying "building your mansion on high" is the truth. It is hard to explain in English, but the heavenly language is pure. There are many ways to say phrases like *well pleased, well done,* and *good job,* and the feeling of what you're saying goes right along with it. It is such a pure language that you know exactly what the meaning is. There is no confusion at all.

The man on the throne was Joseph of Egypt, who had become second in command to Pharaoh himself. This palace was his reward for living righteously on earth, and this is where he chose to live. Every person in heaven may choose their home and surroundings. You can have a palace or a cottage or live in a tent, if that's what makes you happy. You have free access to whatever you like, whatever is most comfortable, and whatever brings you joy. There is never any shortage of anything.

Joseph wore a royal red robe over his Egyptian clothing, and his golden crown resembled a smooth hat that fit his head. The crown wasn't long enough to cover the wisps of flame-red hair that stuck out underneath it. Joseph had a square jaw, a straight nose, well-shaped cheekbones and a slight cleft in his chin. Joseph looked at me with his warm brown eyes and I could see why the Egyptian ladies had found him so handsome.

Then Joseph said to me, "What you did was very noble."

I didn't know if it was his deep voice or the words he spoke that made me go weak in the knees. It wasn't from fear, because I wasn't the least bit afraid of him. I knew that if I wanted to climb up those steps and take a seat on that golden throne, he would be happy to move aside and let me sit there for as long as I wanted to.

Then I realized that the thing that set my heart quivering was a tiny sense of longing in his voice, an echo from his earthly time when his mother died. Then his sorrow was compounded when he was taken from his father, Jacob, by his jealous brothers and sold into slavery. It had all been part of a divine plan, and Joseph had, of course, forgiven his brothers.

Still, he knew what it was like to grow up without a mother to watch over him, and he knew what it was to be robbed of his father's guidance when he was just a young man. Although it had only been in a brief period of his earth life, he truly knew the pains of being orphaned.

Even as my maternal instincts kicked in and my heart went out to him, Joseph's words were hard for me to internalize. I had only done what I did because I wanted to be with my family. I knew that my children needed a mother, and that James couldn't do it on his own. That's all.

After we left Joseph of Egypt, we met with Joshua, the one who fought the battle of Jericho. He stood about eight feet tall and carried himself like a true warrior. He had dark, wavy hair with one unruly brown lock that fell over his forehead. His soulful brown eyes were set deep into his nicely tanned face. If any one man in history had prompted the phrase, "tall, dark and handsome," it would have to be Joshua.

After he shook my hand and told me it was a privilege to meet me, Joshua took me through his city, the City of Plenty. There were huge vegetables twice the size of any other heavenly produce I'd seen so far. The giant vegetables and fruit grew in various places throughout yards and in lots scattered alongside the streets. Grape vines hung heavy with grapes that were easily five times the size of earthly grapes. All their crops were huge, and it was made known to me that even on earth, this culture grew produce that was exceptionally large.

The buildings we passed were made of stone, like the structures from old Roman times. In the center of the city was a courtyard with a stone well. The people in the city didn't need to draw their water from the well anymore, but they'd had one in their city on earth, and they chose to re-create it in heaven. All the houses faced the center court.

There were children playing in the streets, and before I even had a chance to wonder about them, Christ hurried ahead of me to join in their game. As soon as the children caught sight of him, they broke ranks, ran to his side, and threw their arms around him. Each one received a hug before they pulled themselves away and gave Christ a stick so that he could take a turn to hit a rock toward a circle drawn in the dirt. Apparently, whoever got their rock closest to the circle without going inside of it was the winner, but no one seemed to care who "won." It was obvious that they played for the joy of playing, and those whose rocks fell far short of the mark were laughing just as much as those whose rocks stopped right next to the line.

Wow, I thought. *The Lord plays with children.* On second thought, it wasn't so strange to watch him running and laughing with them. It tells us in the scriptures that Jesus loved children, so why would he not want to spend time playing with them? Of course he would.

It came to my mind that these children were ones who had died as children and their spirits retained the age at their death. There were also some who simply had a childlike spirituality. They were waiting for the Millennium in order to continue their progression.

When Christ left the game, he was besieged with good-bye hugs. He finally untangled himself from all the little arms and legs, managing to pat each child on the head or gaze into their eyes and share a kind word with them before he left. The love he had for the little ones radiated from his face as he trotted back to rejoin me, a few children still scampering around him.

Joshua led the way to his palace where he served us a feast of roast lamb, rice, huge succulent vegetables, and plump, sweet fruit.

I stared at the roast lamb, wondering why animals

would be killed when this was heaven. Instantly, I realized that this wasn't a dead lamb at all, but was simply energy formed in whatever shape was desired. All the food was made up of energy, in every shape and flavor anyone wanted. Spirits are made up of energy that is capable of being depleted. While eating is not required to replenish spiritual energy, it is one way that can be used.

I picked up a grape and took a huge bite, but I couldn't fit it all into my mouth. I had to take two more big bites before it was all gone. It was the sweetest, juiciest grape I had ever tasted in my whole life.

The feast was more of a celebration and a community event than nourishment necessary to sustain anyone. The whole town was there—eating, laughing and treating me like a dignitary. I didn't need to be treated like anyone special in order for me to love the time that I spent there. It was easy for me to see why they had made their heaven look like the city they'd lived in on earth.

After saying goodbye to the kind-hearted people in the City of Plenty, we visited the City of Enoch. As soon as we entered the city, I was open-mouthed with awe. Castles made of lead crystal and gold dotted the streets, gleaming softly as they shone with gentle light that seemed to come from within. If you visualize the Salt Lake Temple or a cathedral made of crystal and trimmed with gold, then that is a pretty good image of what the whole city looked like. The streets were paved with shining gold.

As in the other places we had visited, people came out of their homes to meet me. I still thought they were coming for Christ, even though they made a point to shake my hand. A man with pure white hair and the longest beard of pristine white I'd ever seen came up to greet me. It was Enoch himself. The other adults in the city all appeared strong and vibrant, in the prime of their life, but Enoch had chosen to retain the way he looked when he was translated. In spite of his white hair and long beard, he, too, had the vibrance of ideal health and a heart full of love and joy.

The City of Enoch was the largest city I visited, and is full of happy people who are busy and big-hearted, calling friendly greetings to each other as they pass on the streets. Sometimes they stop to talk, and they really, truly listen to what the other person has to say. I was told that this is the way they were on earth and that is why the city was translated. They were all willing to help anyone else whenever they were needed. No one had more goods or resources than anyone else.

That should be our goal here and now, to love one another. There would be no poor, homeless, or anyone in need around us. The people there are as perfect as they were on earth, and I couldn't help but think how great it would be for us to love one another enough to be translated, and not suffer the pains of death by violence or accident or ectopic pregnancy.

I met all the prophets of the Old and New Testaments, as well as a lot of prophets who have no surviving writings on earth. There were a lot more prophets than are recorded in our books of scripture. There have been very few times when there weren't any prophets on earth, because God provided prophets all through time so that people could hear the truth and have the chance to draw closer to him. Father in Heaven's plan cannot be thwarted by the death of his servants or any other means. If someone doesn't fulfill the calling they were sent here to do, then another will be sent. Be assured that the calling will be filled, and the purpose of God will go forward.

I also got to meet the Book of Mormon prophets. Just like the Bible times, there are prophets whose writings have not yet been given to us, but will yet be revealed.

There are too many to tell you about them all, but I will tell you that Nephi is around seven feet tall with well-sculpted muscles, blond hair, blue eyes, and is very handsome. He lives in the heavenly version of a city that the Nephites built after they left an area in the eastern United States. The town was set in flat terrain, perhaps somewhat like Nebraska. Although their houses were simple, round dwellings made of what looked like mud and grass, they were perfectly constructed and beautiful to behold. It's hard to imagine how such simple dwellings can be beautiful, but they were. The Nephites had re-created the city and dwellings where they had been most comfortable on earth, and everyone who wanted to live there was welcomed.

Instead of crooked streets meandering in between structures built randomly throughout the area, they were laid out in precise straight lines, with the neat and simple houses lining the streets. It was a happy place, and I enjoyed meeting the people there.

It's amazing to travel with the Lord. With him leading me, it was a very smooth and easy transition. It's like we never really moved our feet, but in the wink of an eye we were among the Jaredites, in a city that was about ten blocks long and about twelve blocks wide. I stared up in open-mouthed amazement at the height of the Jaredite people. They're about nine feet tall! I was greeted much as I had been before, and felt completely welcome and totally at ease.

There were children playing in the streets of the Jaredite community, too, and again Jesus stopped and played with them. This time it was a game where they kicked a rock. It was an organized game to see who could kick the rock the farthest, with lots of laughter and running about, but I didn't recognize the rules so I couldn't tell who was winning.

Christ obviously did not have the same problem, because he left my side and jumped right in to play with the children. It made me smile to see the joy the children were experiencing, which only rivaled the joy on the Savior's face.

After a few minutes, Jesus stopped his part in the game, turned to me and said, "Come on, it's time to go."

CHAPTER 10

My Favorite Scripture Story Comes Alive

The City of Helaman was about three times larger than the city of the Jaredites, set in the midst of what looked to be a wilderness that resembled the natural landscape of Utah. I noticed sagebrush-like plants and mountains rising in the distance.

The city blocks were laid out in orderly square grids. On the outskirts of the city were charming little houses, not much bigger than my living room, but built with clever workmanship.

The homes were very beautiful but simple dwellings that were selected by their inhabitants. They were like the homes they had loved and been comfortable in on earth.

As I walked with Christ down the street, people came out of their houses to greet us. Jesus turned to me and said, "They're coming to meet you."

My heart protested at the very thought. "But I don't deserve it."

"Yes, you do. Take it." Jesus' voice was soft and reassuring.

The people moved toward me, their smiles bright and their arms outstretched, as welcoming as in any city I'd visited previously. "She's here!" "I see her!" "Let's go meet her!" "Come on, she's here!" It was as though I was a celebrity, when really all I wanted was to be a member of the studio audience.

I noticed that there were certain women dressed in simple woven dresses of unremarkable brown who, when they shook my hand or embraced me, created a peculiar surge of emotion within my heart. I watched them, wondering what it was about them that seemed to tug at my spirit. There was a regal air about them, but not one that put them above anyone else. It was as though they dwelt in a place of high status within their community that, at the same time, did not diminish anyone around them. It was extraordinary.

As soon as I wondered who these women were, I suddenly knew. They were the mothers of the Stripling Warriors, my absolute favorite story from the Book of Mormon, where 2,000 young men went into battle for the sake of their parents who had sworn an oath to never take up arms against their fellow man.

After the battle, not one of the young men had died

from their wounds because their mothers had taught them with unshakable love and unwavering faith that their sons would survive if they were fighting for righteousness and would exercise faith.

I respected and admired the way these mothers kept Christ close enough to their hearts that they could teach their sons about him, with the result that their boys demonstrated amazing faith strong enough to help them survive impossible odds.

A surge of joy so complete that it felt like I was lit from the inside washed through me. How honored I was to meet these women, even as they declared their joy at meeting me.

We arrived at a place on the edge of town where Captain Moroni stood next to Helaman. Moroni was the younger of the two, watching me approach with blue eyes full of merriment underneath a shock of dark blond hair.

Helaman glanced at me with warm brown eyes, and in that instant I knew that I could trust my life to this man. He took my hand in his and smiled. I felt a connection with him, as though he was a favorite uncle, the fun kind that teases and plays catch with you until you've had enough, then treats you to ice cream before taking you home.

Moroni was impatient for his turn to greet me. Where Helaman had pressed my hand between his palms, Moroni pumped my arm up and down with youthful energy.

"Here's a real, truly genuine, pleased-to-meet-you handshake," he said. "Not an old man squeeze-the-hand greeting."

"Who are you calling an old man?" Helaman said in mock severity. He turned his head from side to side. "I don't see any old men around here."

In truth, both Helaman and Moroni looked to be the same age. It was only the depth of the look in their eyes that seemed to reveal a difference in age, or maybe it was a difference in their basic personalities that made one seem younger and one older.

I soon discovered that Helaman and Moroni had a long-standing habit of teasing and joking with each other, but underneath their jovial words was a solid layer of determination to protect whatever or whoever they were sent to guard. Moroni's calling on earth was largely to protect the people he lived among, and he still exuded the attitude of a big brother watching out for his younger siblings.

I noticed that there were tents scattered around among the sagebrush that crept up to the edges of town. These were no ordinary tents. They looked as if they were made out of spun gold. It was astounding to me that even the camping gear in heaven is exquisite!

I turned back from the tents to see Moroni and

Helaman pulling themselves up to attention at the head of a double column of incredible-looking young men. My heart melted. I knew in an instant that these were the Stripling Warriors. Their hair was varying shades of blonde and brunette. Some had blue eyes, while the eyes of others were brown. All the warriors were well over six feet tall, with muscled arms as big around as a man's thigh, and well-defined washboard stomachs.

As Jesus and I walked down the corridor of warriors standing at attention with their eyes straight ahead, I was impressed by their reverent demeanor for our Savior. Again, the thought came from Jesus to me, "No, this is for you."

From behind me, I could hear Moroni chuckle. "She doesn't know this is for her."

I looked back over my shoulder as Helaman said, "No, she doesn't understand the greatness of her decision," but his mouth didn't move. I was reading Helaman's thoughts to Moroni. By now I was getting used to people thinking things to me instead of saying them, but since Moroni and Helaman were talking to one another, I didn't understand why I "heard" what they were saying.

Then it came to me that there can be no gossip in heaven. If someone is thinking something about you, then you can pick it up. If they're not thinking about you, then you don't catch it. Simple as that.

"This is because of what you did," Helaman said, catching my eye.

"For the intent of your heart," added Moroni. They sure didn't sound like they were joking.

I couldn't believe it. I felt so unworthy of all this attention, even though walking the ranks of all 2,000 of the Stripling Warriors was the highlight of my experience. I admired them and their mothers so much, and hoped that I could do even half as well with my own children.

CHAPTER 11

Old Nauvoo and
Old Salt Lake City

S ome saints who loved the old city of Nauvoo chose
to live in the spiritual Nauvoo in heaven. Since
that was the happiest place that Joseph and Emma
Smith had lived on earth, that's where they make their
heavenly home, too.

As we entered the city, I caught the delightful
aroma of freshly baked bread. We passed picket fences
skirted with lovely old-fashioned flowers popular 160
years ago, such as velvet roses, cheerful hollyhocks, and
bright daisies, dressed in glorious colors and blessed
with perfect proportions.

The city was organized in square blocks, and I
glimpsed gardens in many of the backyards. I noticed
some ripe red tomatoes peering out from between
fuzzy green leaves. It came to my mind that if people
enjoyed gardening, then they grew a garden. If they

didn't want to, they didn't have to. They were free to choose whatever activities they liked.

Boys rolled hoops down the street, and girls jumped rope and played on hopscotch squares scratched into the dirt. By now I wasn't one bit surprised when Christ left my side and hurried to join their games. After greeting the children, he took a turn at hopscotch, and then jumped a long rope spun by a girl on each end, singing the old jump rope chant along with the children as he skipped nimbly over the turning rope.

My pioneer ancestors stepped forward from the ranks of my family who still followed me through heaven. They conducted tours for me of the homes they'd occupied in their mortal existence in Nauvoo. It was great fun to see where they'd lived.

Joseph Smith came out of his house to welcome us, seeming as delighted to see me again as he was at first, although there were no back flips this time around. I realized that he looked much more handsome in person than in any of his pictures I had ever seen. When you view a painting of him, it seems that the nose is one of his most prominent features. Especially in viewing his death mask, there is no animation, and it doesn't do his features any justice at all. Yet when he's talking and smiling and laughing, then his nose fits his face perfectly and his electric blue eyes sparkle with merriment and good will.

Emma invited us to eat with them. As in Joseph's case, there are no pictures that do justice to Emma's beauty. She is an extremely beautiful woman.

We sat down to a meal of roasted chicken, biscuits, corn on the cob and mashed potatoes with gravy. Again, there was no actual dead chicken sitting on the table. It was all energy formed and flavored in whatever way the diners wished.

The corn and potatoes were from Emma's own garden, and it seems that the Lord is particularly fond of sweet potato pie, so Emma had plenty of that on hand for dessert.

Joseph loves to talk and he kept up a lively conversation during the whole meal. At one point he stopped and stared at me. With a mischievous grin, he said, "I can't believe that you told Christ 'no.' Amazing."

As I gazed into Joseph Smith's merry eyes, it came to my understanding that he doesn't see himself as a martyr. He doesn't know why he is sometimes aggrandized on earth, because he only did what he came to do. In the same light, we all want to worship and praise Jesus Christ, yet he only wants us to love one another. That will please him more than any other worship there could ever be. Christ is love and that is all. There is no pride anywhere in him. Christ was ultimately kind to me, and there was never a time when he took any glory from my actions, he gave it all to me during our heavenly visits, even though I didn't think that what I did was worth all the hoo-ha. Christ is the kindest and meekest man who ever lived.

Once we were through eating, Emma turned to me and said with a smile, "I love this part." She snapped her fingers over the table, and every dirty dish and cup and fork and scrap of leftover food broke into little particles as though they were in the *Star Trek* transporter. Then the particles vanished.

I was astounded. It instantly came to my mind that in heaven, you don't have to wash the dishes if you don't want to. The first tinge of jealousy I'd felt since passing over flashed through my heart, because I love being with my children, but it's the laundry and dishes that I can't keep up with

Not to be outdone, my Nauvoo ancestor families invited me to eat at their houses, too. Since eating is more a social event than to soothe hunger, I ate at each of my relatives' homes who invited me, simply enjoying our time together. The neat thing was, I never felt hungry and I never got too full. I always felt just right.

Grandma Burton invited me to go with her and see her house, which was fashioned after the one I'd visited when she lived on earth in Afton, Wyoming. Her house was just the same as I remembered it, only everything was shiny and new. It probably looked like it had in its prime in the 1930s. She had her cook stove sitting in the middle of her kitchen and bread baking in the oven, a familiar sight and smell from my childhood. At the sight of that well-loved place, the memories came flooding back, and I felt the same love that I'd felt when visiting there as a child.

Since Grandma always made sure that we were well fed whenever we were at her house, she made sure that I had a slice of warm bread with melted butter before I left. Grandpa Burton was right behind me, patiently waiting for his piece. Grandma made sure to give a slice of fresh bread to Christ, too.

Next, Grandpa Scholes showed me his apartment. I was surprised that it was small and sparsely furnished, not one bit like the house he'd lived in on earth.

Before I could even ask him, Grandpa said, "This is my little bachelor pad." He winked at me, and I was sure he could read the confusion on my face. "I'm waiting for your grandma to get here so we can build our home in heaven together." Grandpa slid his arm around me. "Don't you worry about me for one minute, Suzie, I'm perfectly happy with this place. Besides, I'm hardly ever here anyway. I'm usually on assignment to help the grandkids who are serving their church missions in mortality."

I shared a warm hug with Grandpa, grateful to

know that he would be a companion to my children when they were old enough to serve missions.

The next place I visited was Brigham Young's Beehive House. It is set in an old Salt Lake City that must mirror the way the town appeared in the late 1850s, about ten years after the Saints arrived in the Rocky Mountains. It is a wonderful, bustling city, with unpaved streets and people striding from place to place with purpose.

There is much happiness there, along with a boundless sense of freedom carried over to heaven from when the Saints established themselves in the Great Salt Lake Valley on earth.

The Beehive House in the spirit world is new and beautiful. A lot of people stop by to visit with Brigham Young. From some of the things I'd read about him, I used to think that we would not get along. For some reason, I thought that he might be kind of a tough guy, with blunt speech and brusque manners, but I actually found him to be very kind. He's not as stern as I had imagined. He simply can't hide the tender qualities of his personality. He was gracious, and greeted me like a gentleman would greet a lady.

He made sure we were served an energy meal formed as roast beef, beets, fresh homemade bread, mashed potatoes and gravy, and tender apple pie for dessert.

As I ate, I couldn't help but wonder about all of Brigham Young's wives. It was made known to me that he loves all of his wives, and treats them as differently as their individual personalities, yet with equal love and respect.

After supper, he took me into the main living room, the long one just to the east of the front door on the south side of the Beehive House. People would enter through that door when they visited Brigham on earth. In that room, I was privileged to meet the deceased prophets of this dispensation. Besides Brigham Young, there was John Taylor, Wilford Woodruff, Lorenzo Snow, Joseph F. Smith, Heber J. Grant, George Albert Smith, David O. McKay, Joseph Fielding Smith, Harold B. Lee, Spencer W. Kimball, Ezra Taft Benson, and Howard W. Hunter.

Even though each one introduced himself to me, it felt like I already knew them. I enjoyed shaking all of their hands, but it was especially rewarding to meet the prophets who had lived on earth during my lifetime.

As I left the Beehive House, many of my pioneer ancestors stepped forward. These men and women had made the trek across the plains and helped build Salt Lake City. They showed me the homes they had lived in on earth.

Even though in an earthly timeline, the Salt Lake Temple had hardly been started ten years after the

Saints' arrival, it was standing resplendent in the Salt Lake City of heaven.

I was shown all of the temples, and I was told that any dwelling or place dedicated by the priesthood on earth has an exact replica in heaven.

CHAPTER 12

The Founding Fathers

We soon moved to another part of the spirit world, and with Christ at my side, I walked up the steps of an old capital building that had been built before the White House was even thought of. We entered a broad corridor with a wide-planked hardwood floor, polished to a high sheen. Voices came from a room off to one side. When we pushed open the door, I saw George Washington standing at a podium, addressing the signers of the Declaration of Independence.

He looked up when we entered, then smiled and came over to greet us. George Washington stands nearly 6' 4" and has broad shoulders. He's a quiet and gentle man, but he's firm in things that matter. He's a deep thinker blessed with a gift to know just what to do in order to get the job done. The affection between George Washington and Christ was quite evident, and it was reassuring to me to see that the first president of the United States is very close to the Lord.

After introducing me to George Washington, Christ went around the room with me to meet Benjamin Franklin, Thomas Jefferson, John Adams, and all the rest of the Founding Fathers of the United States of America. They were all quite pleased to meet me, and Christ beamed at my side. His brotherly affection was quite evident for all of them.

Abraham Lincoln strode into the room on his long legs, leading a procession of all the righteous presidents of the United States. Abraham Lincoln is a kind and considerate, with gentlemanly ways salted with just the right dash of wit and humor.

The founding fathers and former leaders of our country let me know that they are grieved at the state of our country. They fought hard to retain our freedom for future generations, and they told me that we're throwing it away. They asked me to get the message out to everyone I could reach that we should stand up for our rights and never allow them to be taken away, or else they would be the fathers of a forgotten nation. They put their whole hearts and souls into the forming of this country, the writing of the Declaration of Independence and establishing the Constitution. Every one of them either gave their life or would have willingly laid their life down in order to make sure that 230 years later we would still have the rights and privileges that they wanted us to have and enjoy.

They are deeply saddened to see the rampant wickedness in our country today. They were righteous men during their time on earth. They raised their voices with intense passion to tell me how afraid they are for the future of the United States. "If you take God out of our country, then God won't stay where he's not wanted. If Americans do not start living righteously and put God back in, then the country will be taken from them."

With tears in their eyes, they told me how hard they'd worked to set up a place of freedom, how deeply they believe in the United States of America, and how in their day they would never have allowed God to be taken out of the country, either in reference or with any kind of action that would disallow calling upon God at any time. They urged me to let others know that we must stand up and not permit this to happen any more.

I learned that the United States of America deserves whichever president is in office. If we are not living Godlike lives as a nation, we will not have a Godlike president. If we take God out of our schools, he will not stay where he is not invited.

I was told that if we do not put God back into all aspects of our life, whether it be in our own separate life or as a nation, we will not be a free nation anymore, and the heavens will weep.

Some of these righteous men who were early leaders of the United States are incensed about the immoral stories that are circulating about them. There are many stories of the founding fathers not acting in a godlike manner. These stories aren't true.

It's no coincidence that many of the men who helped shape the United States were self-appointed teetotalers and also refrained from smoking in a day and age when no health problems or social taboos were associated with it. Patrick Henry even concocted a non-alcoholic barley drink that he offered for sale in his store as an effort to encourage men to abandon their whiskey.

In 1787, Ben Franklin attended the Constitutional Convention in spite of the fact that he was sometimes in great pain and had to be carried to the meetings in a sedan chair. At one point, he humbly asked the assembly to consider prayer before debating issues important to the future of the country. He reminded the assembly that in the war with Britain, their prayers were answered. "The longer I live, the more convincing proofs I see of this truth, that God governs in the affairs of men. I therefore beg leave to move that, henceforth, prayers imploring the assistance of heaven and its blessing on our deliberations be held in this assembly every morning before we proceed to business."

When Benjamin Franklin signed The Declaration of Independence at age 81, he wept with emotion.

At the impressionable age of eleven, the mortal George Washington learned from his dying father's bedside that he should never misuse his physical power, which was considerable. Washington offered frequent prayers throughout his life and acknowledged over 60 desperate moments during the struggle for independence when he would have suffered disaster had not the hand of God intervened. It was during prayer one day when he had a vision of the birth, progress, and destiny of the United States.

John Adams credited the powers of heaven for throwing him and the other men who helped form the United States into existence at the same time.

Thomas Jefferson drafted the Declaration of Independence without use of any reference documents. The Declaration states in part, "Governments are instituted among men, deriving their just powers from the consent of the governed." If Americans ever come to believe that their rights and freedoms are instituted by politicians, then they will grovel before them, seeking favors. Since God created man, who in turn created government, it follows that man is superior to government and should remain master over it.

Jefferson submitted the bill for "Establishing Religious Freedom in Virginia," affirming that no church would be supported by taxes. This "separation of church and state" was not intended to imply that religion was unimportant in the affairs of men, but only that government could not interfere with religious activity.

Just before taking a prescribed dose of liquid mercury, which the physician stated would either kill him or cure him, Patrick Henry excused himself to pray for the welfare of his family, his country, and his own soul. The mercury proved fatal, and the patriotic lawyer left behind a will that split his earthly assets among his family, then mentioned that the religion of Christ would make them rich indeed.

This only illustrates a few acts done by some of these inspired men while living on earth. All of the 56 men who signed the Declaration of Independence were at one time or another the victims of manhunts, and were driven from their homes. Seventeen lost everything they owned, twelve had their homes burned to the ground, nine died as a result of the Revolutionary War, five were brutally treated as prisoners of war, at least two had to suffer the pains of seeing their wives abused, and many of them lost family members, some even their entire families.

They did what was asked of them by God. They were all God-fearing and did what was appropriate in their day. None of them would have knowingly done anything against God's will.

CHAPTER 13

The Last Days and The Book of Life

Even though I was shown portions of the Last Days, I choose not to dwell on that. The prophets have testified of it over the years, and there is no need for me to go into detail.

I will say that if the food is shared in gratitude, with no selfishness, then the pot will always be full. The wheat bucket will never run out. When you take some out and share it, then the next time you open the bucket, it will be as though the wheat was never used.

We can be saved by thinking of pure love, extending loving thoughts to others, by having grateful hearts, and by exercising faith in God.

Also, do not be afraid. Fear attracts desolation to anyone who holds it in their hearts. Letting go of fear will protect us in the last days. If we are prepared, we will not fear. Christ is always willing to help us if we only ask. Be grateful for everything, even in adversity.

I also know that the future is altered by the choices we make. For example, if my husband James were to take a job in New York and we moved our family there, then my life would be different because of the choice we made to take a new job and move. We'd meet new people and travel a different path then we're currently on. It's the same with people as a whole. When a community decides to act in one way or another, it changes the course of their future. It's the same for the last days. Our actions and thoughts as people of earth will determine the timing and events of the last days.

Negativity can bring on and harbor illness. When you allow negative thoughts to enter your mind, it brings in the adversary. Lucifer has power if we let him, but Christ's power is always greater.

Christ took me into a room lined floor to ceiling with books as white as milk. A high table sat in the center of the room. Christ moved over to one wall and pulled a book with a cover like pearl from its place on the shelf. It was huge, about three feet long and two feet wide. It had a binding like the big old books in the basements of a library or city hall, only it was much cleaner than any book that sat on an earthly shelf. Christ seated himself on a stool and laid the spotless book on the high table before him. He opened the pages, pulled out a pen the color of new snow, and began to write.

"In this book, I am writing of the perfect love you have for your children," he said. I was in awe. I knew a lot of mothers who would have done just the same thing I did.

I must emphasize to everyone how much Christ loves it when we love one another, and lose ourselves in the service of others. I really didn't think it was necessary to write about my one act of refusing to go with him, because I still didn't feel it was noteworthy.

Everyone has a story in this book, and it's a privilege to be in Christ's presence while he writes. Every good deed is noticed, but on the other hand, every bad deed that is not repented of is noticed and recorded, too. But when repentance is complete, the incident is wiped clean, as if it never happened.

It was made known to me that anyone can have any of the spiritual gifts if they ask for them. You need to do all in your power to achieve them, such as living up to the things you know you should do. Then ask for the gifts that you desire, and believe that you will receive. The Book of Mormon counsels that we should desire spiritual gifts and seek after them.

First and foremost should be the gift of discernment, because it's so easy to be deceived when you seek the gifts of the spirit.

Some people go to mediums for fortune telling, but that is not the Lord's way. He would prefer that we seek for individual inspiration through prayer.

When Christ was done writing, he took me into a beautiful room of white-on-white walls and soft drapes of the purest white. He sat me down on a cloud-soft chair, face to face with him. He told me that since I had now seen his face, I am to testify of him. I need to teach of his love, kindness, and the mercy that he has for all of us. Whenever he teaches one, he tells them to teach others whenever the spirit prompts, and not to keep the knowledge hidden.

Now this is part of my life, to teach others of Christ's amazing love for all of us, and how deeply he desires all of us to return to him.

CHAPTER 14

The Reassigned Children

Christ took me back to the gardens of heaven, and I sensed that it was nearing time for me to return to earth. While I had every intention of going back, my heart sagged at the very thought. Not only would I miss all the beauty in heaven—including the ease of cleaning up after dinner—but I would have to return to a body that would be suffering from a painful miscarriage. That wasn't even the worst of it. More agonizing than that would be my empty arms with no baby to hold.

I'd always had an early emotional attachment to my unborn babies, feeling a sense of unbounded joy when I first found out I was carrying them. I always wondered what they would be like, what they would look like, and eagerly anticipated their arrival. I had already felt that this baby was a very real part of our family, and now she would be gone. I didn't know how I would bear the loss.

A calming presence moved into my circle of awareness, and I looked up from my dreary thoughts to see Jesus' earthly mother, Mary, standing in front of me. Dark hair framed her lovely face, and her blue eyes regarded me with such compassion that tears stung my eyes. She put her arms out and embraced me, wrapping me not only in warmth but a soft and comforting layer of empathy.

Mary took my hand and walked with me along a pathway that ended up close to where I had started. Mary didn't stop until we'd entered a pretty white gazebo with delicate woodwork that looked like Victorian lace trimming the eaves. She lowered herself onto a bench and patted the seat beside her. I sat down.

The spirit of my little daughter who'd been my ectopic pregnancy joined us. In fact, her spirit had tagged along with me for most of my journey through heaven, sometimes stopping to play with the children we encountered, only to catch up with me later. She had also milled about with my other family members. Since I'd always wanted to have a daughter named BrookLynn Rose, I called this little girl Brook.

"It is such a noble thing to be a mother," Mary said to me, her liquid blue eyes filled with sympathy. "I can understand your pain." There was no question in my mind that she understood perfectly.

"It will just be so hard to return knowing that my

little one won't be with me," I said. "My empty arms would be the most painful thing to endure."

Brook skipped over and wrapped her arms around me in a brief hug, then scampered off again. I watched her go. "After the damage done by the ectopic pregnancy, I don't know if I can even have any more children. It's hard to lose Brook. I'll miss her so much." The very real possibility of sudden and permanent sterility hit me, and I quailed at the thought.

Mary put a tender and reassuring hand over mine as her gaze followed Brook's antics across the grass. Mary's amazing blue eyes were soft with compassion. Since her love is so great, she often attends little children on earth as a guardian angel.

Mary turned back to me, her face breathtaking in its beauty. "There's this place," Mary said, then paused. "I'll see if I can get permission. Wait here a moment." Mary stood and glided off across the grass.

Brook dashed into the gazebo and sat in Mary's place. I looked into her eyes, and she gazed back at me with a twinkle in her eye. She was such a beautiful child, and I already felt a deep love for her. She looked like a mix of the features of all three of my girls. From the mischievous expression on her face, I was fairly sure that I knew the answer already, but I still had to ask the question that burned my tongue.

"Do you want to come back?" I asked.

Brook shook her head. "I have to stay." She patted my hand, and I was comforted. I knew that Brook had made the right choice.

It was made known to me that sometimes a miscarriage is allowed as a challenge for the mother or family, and the brief time spent in the mother's womb has fulfilled that particular spirit's mission. Sometimes a miscarriage occurs because there is a problem with the DNA or some other facet of development, and the spirit that would have claimed that body may come again.

Depending on the cause and purpose of the event, miscarried babies may be able to choose whether the miscarriage is their total earthly experience, or whether they want to go again. Brook appeared to be having too much fun to want to wait around for an earthly nine months to give it another go. Besides, she had said she had to stay, and in my heart of hearts, I knew it was the right thing for her to do.

This choice is only offered to those spirits who miscarry. In the case of abortion, the baby's agency is taken away, and those spirits are taken to the reassigned children area. What was shared with me is that since the choice was taken from them, then they will have another chance. They need to have the right to experience life and fulfill their mission on earth as was planned in the grand council in the pre-mortal world. That was and is the reason for the atonement; choice and accountability.

I want to make sure that it's understood that this is not reincarnation. Even in The Church of Jesus Christ of Latter-day Saints, we do not seal a child to the parents if the baby has not taken a breath of life. If an infant has taken the breath of life, that means they chose that body as their own, and even if the baby only lives for a few seconds, that spirit will not be coming back again to take another body. Their choice has already been made.

In reincarnation, it is believed that we come over and over again until we get it right. But the whole reason for Christ's role on earth is the Atonement, so that we don't have to keep trying and trying. As I was taught, Christ died so we might live. If he died so we might live, and live, and live, and keep on living over and over, then why did he die? If we could get it right eventually, then why would we need Jesus Christ or his Atonement? If we keep coming back over and over, there is no need for spirit prison or paradise. What about when we are resurrected? Since there is not a hair of the head which shall be lost, then which body would we choose? There would be no reason for the resurrection.

There is no such thing as reincarnation. You deny the Atonement ever happened if you believe in multiple mortalities. Can you imagine Heavenly Father saying, "You failed this life so now you have to live another one with no memory?" How do you know what test you failed the previous time if you have no memory? It simply doesn't make sense.

If people have memories of times from before, then they most likely saw that time when they were a spirit. Since we can sometimes watch what happens on earth from the pre-mortal world, then some people may carry memories of things that happened before their time on earth, and mistakenly think it's reincarnation. Perhaps they acted as guardian angels in certain places or for certain people, and their vague memories of that time make them think they were reincarnated.

Family members and friends can act as guardian angels to help us return to God's kingdom. After we pass to the other side, our mission may be to help others on earth return to our Heavenly Father.

Guardian angels are never too busy to help when we need it. All we have to do is ask in righteousness and we can get help. Father in Heaven wants all of us to live with him. That's why there are guardian angels, spirit guides, and heavenly guardians. When we think or talk of them, they are there, faster than a phone call. If you learn to listen, they can talk to you and give you guidance from the other side. You can rest assured that those loved ones who have passed are helping us here on earth. They receive their greatest joy in seeing good things that we are doing; however, their greatest sadness is when they see us become worldly, selfish or cruel. If we turn away from righteous living, they will leave, because they do not like evil.

Mary came walking back toward me, her lovely features turned up into a smile. Hyrum Smith was close behind her, and he spoke before Mary did.

"I heard," Hyrum said, his eyes alight with joy, "and I know the perfect one for you."

"The perfect one what?"

"Child. You get to choose one of the reassigned children."

Hyrum pulled me to my feet. He must have sensed my confusion, because he and Mary explained to me that reassigned children are those spirits who are aborted or who are prevented in some way from joining those families who had promised in pre-mortal life to have them.

Children who are spontaneously aborted by women who get pregnant and then intentionally misuse drugs or other substances harmful to their bodies also end up in the reassigned children area.

Joseph and Emma Smith joined us along the way. They love to go to the reassigned children area, and often visit simply to spend time playing with the children.

The flowers in the reassigned children are bright, eager primary colors of red, yellow and blue, quite different from the flowers I'd seen around the temples which were a soft, glowing white. I thought back to other places where flowers had been muted pastels, and still others where they were as vibrant as flame. It seemed that the flowers matched the purpose of the building or place where they grew, and carried the mood of holiness, playfulness, happiness or tranquility. The flowers of heaven are an integral part of the place, lending an aura of quiet beauty as they vibrate with life.

Another thing I admired about the flowers of heaven is that any time a flower is picked, a new one appears in its place.

The reassigned children area is one of the most beautiful places in heaven, with terraced landscaping of three different levels spilling over with beautiful gardens of various plants. The children are permitted to play wherever they want to. It's a joyous and happy place, and it is Christ's favorite place to be. Many people in heaven count it among their favorite spots.

The children appear to range in age from toddlers to pre-teens. They are pure and full of love, and they never fight or quarrel.

On top of a small hill with soft grass that whispers an invitation to roll down is a playground with everything a child would love to have; swings, slides, merry go rounds, monkey bars, everything. There were also grassy knolls scattered around where children could play if they wanted to.

As soon as the children caught sight of Christ, they ran to him, laughing. Christ broke away from me and surprised me by darting away from the children, the transparent cloak that he wore over his white robe flying out behind him. I understood his reason as soon as he turned to look over his shoulder at the miniature crowd hard on his heels, his face alight with joy to see that they were keeping up the chase.

I figured that Christ must be able to run faster than he was actually going, but his real intention was not to outrun his pursuers. Sure enough, before long, one of the children grabbed onto his cloak and Christ tumbled down onto a patch of grass, landing in a heap. The children piled on top of him, shrieking with delight.

After the chase, Christ played ball, swung on the swing set, and hung from tree branches with the children. Laughter bubbled through the air.

Between some of the trees were open spaces where I saw children being taught. Many schoolteachers choose to go to the reassigned children area after they pass on, because their love for teaching goes with them into the next world. This is the beauty of heaven- you do what you're good at and what you enjoyed on earth.

The only time sadness overshadows the reassigned children's place is when an aborted child's spirit arrives. It may take a little while for the spirit to adjust, but it soon realizes that it will be happier with a new family. Not only does the aborted child go to the reassigned children place, but also all those who will be that child's descendents. For example, if one of the spirits were to have four children, then each of them had four children that would be sixteen in just one more generation. Then each of them had four children would equal 64 in the great-grandchildren level, and so on, and so on. See how it multiplies? They all go to the reassigned children area! The blessings last to the eternities, and when a child is chosen, a whole generation goes with him or her.

There was one light-haired little boy playing in the flowers. As soon as he saw Hyrum and Joseph, he jumped up and dropped the flowers that he held in his hand. The blossoms tumbled toward the grass. To my astonishment, as soon as they touched the ground, they disappeared.

The boy jumped straight into Hyrum's arms. It was plain to see that the two had a great deal of affection for one another.

Hyrum turned a beaming face toward me. "This is the boy," he said.

"You'd be a good mother for him," Christ added.

The child was absolutely charming, and I knew that since Hyrum loved him so much, and with Christ's approval, it would be easy for me to love him, too. After watching all the children laughing and playing, I was grateful to have help in choosing one, because they were all so beautiful and radiant that I couldn't have done it on my own. I trusted the choice of the heavenly beings for the child that would be ideal for me, and that in return, our home would be the best one to provide the earth life experience that he needed. Knowing that this child would be coming made the prospect of returning to earth easier on my heart.

When the little boy and I embraced one another, all of the other reassigned children cheered for joy. There was not even a shred of jealousy, no whining, and no cries of, "That's not fair!" Everyone was happy for him, and I could sense the excitement they had for their friend who would now have a chance to experience life on earth. I sensed a joyous anticipation from some of the assembled children for the time when it would be their turn to go. Eighteen months later that boy turned out to be our son, Wesley Hyrum.

I was able to see one child actually leave for his new earthly home. It was quite a send-off, even more joyous than when I chose my new son. I loved being in that place, and felt like I could have stayed there forever.

As I wondered about the children around me, it

was made known that some of the children waiting in the reassigned children area were spirits with special missions who had been promised by particular parents that they would have them in order for the child to carry out his earthly purpose. But the parents had somehow lost track of the thread that tied them to their pre-mortal agreements and had chosen to limit their families, or else made their bodies unfit or unable to conceive and bear a child.

Some couples had their sights set on a bigger, more expensive house and didn't have room in the budget for more children—or even one child—and some wanted to travel or were wrapped up in a career that would be inconvenienced by having children. Others had started taking drugs out of curiosity or in an effort to find a "quick fix" for temporary earthly trials. For whatever reason, they didn't end up with the children they had promised to have.

The spirits that are discarded by earthly parents will be reassigned. Since God is over all, everything will ultimately work out to achieve His purposes, but the original promise is broken, and the line of descendents for the family that didn't fulfill their promise is given to another. There are great consequences for not having the family you promised to have, and there are great blessings for taking on reassigned children and having more than you covenanted for.

This is not to say that families must have 30 or 40 children in order to be in good standing! Certainly not. Please do not agonize over the number of children you have—or don't have—even though this can amount to emotional torture for childless couples who suffer the heart-breaking trial of not being able to bear their own children. Christ knows their pain, and he suffers along with them. There are reasons as varied as there are spirits for this to happen. God's ways are not man's ways, and he has his own reasons for not sending reassigned children to couples who yearn for children, yet have none. No matter what, his intense love for every single one of his children is steady and unwavering. Some people are meant to get the children they're supposed to raise through adoption.

Some people on earth only have one or two children, but it's not for lack of willingness or desire to have more. Then there are others who can only handle a certain number of children because of limits on their emotional, physical, or mental health.

What it boils down to is that we *must not* judge one another. Regardless of the reasons for people's life situations, we all value our own agency to choose, and must grant the same privilege to others. In many cases, the couples do not choose their childless situation, and it is cruel to ask them why they aren't having children. Guard diligently against any thoughtless comments you may unwittingly make to childless couples or those with fewer children than you *think* they should have. We are supposed to love and help one another, not lecture and sit in judgment. Be anxiously engaged in truly loving and helping one another, and be concerned only with correcting your own shortcomings and weaknesses.

Each child of God can search his or her own heart in earnest prayer and receive the answers that pertain to their own lives.

CHAPTER 15

The Living Waters

Off in the distance, I noticed the glint from the surface of a dazzling lake that appeared to be made of liquid silver. I was intrigued and wanted to get a closer look. Then *phing!* I was there, standing at the water's edge and looking down through water so clear I could count the grains of sand that shifted lazily on the bottom.

How had I gotten there so fast? It was as though I'd been led by Christ's own hand, except that when I traveled with him at the speed of thought, it was a smooth ride. When I tried it myself, it was rather jerky, kind of like an inexperienced pilot trying to land an airplane. Still, it was the first time I was instantly somewhere on my own, and I found it to be great fun. I was losing my mortality mindset, since I was allowing myself to travel like the people in heaven did.

A river gurgled merrily into the lake, forming ripples on the silvery surface. I cupped my hand, dipped it into the water, and brought up a handful of shimmering silver. With mounting wonder, I passed the moist ball back and forth from hand to hand. It's sort of like mercury, but much better. It's like a liquid and a solid at the same time. Since there is nothing like it on earth, it's hard to explain.

Have you ever mixed water and cornstarch? If you get the correct proportions, when you hold the mixture in your hand, it can drip through you fingers, but when you strike it, it feels like a solid. This water was just the opposite. Running your hands through it was smooth and easy, but when I picked up a handful, it formed a damp silver ball in my fingers.

"Go ahead and renew yourself in the Living Waters," Christ said as he came up beside me. He didn't have to tell me twice. I jumped in and swam through the amazing element, delighted to discover that I felt completely weightless. It was almost like I was floating in air, but I could propel myself through the water with my arms and legs. I discovered some beautifully sculpted coral, and swam around it as free as a mermaid.

The notion brushed my mind that I was underwater, yet I didn't feel any need to surface for air. "I don't have to take a breath!" I thought, luxuriating in the water beside the coral bed. Amused, I swam around with complete ease, the silver yet transparent water holding me up with a touch so light, it was as though it wasn't even there. I swam and played like a kid in a swimming pool.

As I wondered at this marvelous substance, it came to my mind that angels often swim in the Living Waters in order to renew and refresh themselves. Angels assigned to guard mortals need periodic rest and tranquility. I was pleased to discover that there are many ways to renew your spirit in heaven, depending on what you feel like doing at the time.

When I climbed out of the water, I felt the absolute best I'd ever felt in my life.

I walked over to a magnificent tree and settled myself on the ground beneath it in order to ponder my situation. I was mesmerized by this glorious place, and although I never changed my mind into thinking I would stay, I almost wanted to. It is so peaceful and pretty in heaven that I knew I would miss it so much my heart would ache.

It felt very much like when you move out of a house that you have lived in for many years, a place full of good memories, love, and laughter, and you really don't want to go, even though you know that moving is the right thing. I wanted to go back to be with my children, because they'd be traveling different paths than had been agreed upon if I stayed on this side of the veil.

Feelings are felt more strongly on earth in our physical bodies than in heaven with just our spirits. That's why we all wanted to go to earth, in order to really feel the pain and the contrasting joy that is possible to feel.

I wondered about guardian angels watching over my children, and it was made known to me that angels are waiting to drop everything they're doing and help us if we just ask. Their main goal is to help those on earth to get back to Heavenly Father, so they'll do anything they can to help.

If we have a problem with something, we can ask the Lord for assistance, and he'll either help us or send someone who can. Guaranteed. All you need is to have faith, and to believe that it's going to work. That's not really so hard when you consider the many stories in the scriptures of healing, the accounts of walking on water, and feeding thousands of people with a small amount of food. The scriptures are full of miracles. We just have to believe miracles can happen to us, too.

Angels protect children, who don't have as much of a veil as adults do. Some children can even see their angels, and call them imaginary friends. Most children on earth wouldn't make it to adulthood without guardian angels.

It grieves the heavens that there are people who exercise their agency to harm those who are smaller and weaker than they are. Although it is hard to see this abuse, all things will be made right in the end.

Sometimes people get sick and hurt on earth just because it's part of their experience. Sometimes we suffer because it's what we came here to do. Bad things happen to good people, and there are valuable lessons to be learned from these experiences.

Whenever things go "wrong" in my life, I never recognize Lucifer as the instigator. Whether he caused the problem or not, he loves to get the credit for anything that happens that upsets us, angers us, or makes our lives hard. I never acknowledge him for anything, because he sees it as glory, so I just let the experience go and move on.

People don't usually ask for enough help. You can ask for heavenly help for anything, but I think there's a point where you can ask for too much. I once heard of a man who prayed about which brand of canned beans to buy at the store. It's all right for him to do this if it makes him feel better, I'm not one to judge his individual situation, but the way I see it is that we are supposed to be learning and growing and taking some responsibility for ourselves on this earth. I think we ought to use our free agency to make a lot of our own choices.

CHAPTER 16

Going Away Party

Jesus knew my thoughts and understood perfectly that I was having a hard time about leaving. He sat on the ground under the tree beside me, and covered my hand with his. I looked down to see the cruel scar in the back of his hand, the one from the spike that had nailed him to a wooden cross. His voice was infinitely kind when he said, "I can remove your memories of being here, but you must know that you may never get them back. If they do return, it will be in bits and pieces, and it will take effort on your part to retrieve them."

I looked up from his strong hand and into his compassionate gaze. I knew myself well enough to be certain that it would be difficult enough for me to go back to my stretch-marked body that would now bear fresh surgery stitches. To think of having to maintain any semblance of a cheerful mood in mortality with my mind full of memories of this idyllic place was unthinkable. How could I go back to the pain of recovery and also deal with the pain of losing the constant peace that cloaked me in heaven?

I knew I would have a hard time. Although I can tolerate pain if I have to, I do not like it and avoid it as much as possible. So I took Christ up on his offer.

Christ helped me up, and I accepted hugs from friends and family who knew the time was fast approaching for me to leave.

One handsome young man in a dark suit who looked vaguely familiar encircled me with his arms. When he pulled back, he glanced at my perplexed face and let out a laugh.

"You don't know me, do you?" he teased.

"No, well, maybe I do, but I don't quite remember," I confessed.

"I'm your nephew George," he said, grinning.

I wondered if I was losing my memory. "I don't have a nephew named George."

George lifted a finger and shook it playfully in my direction. "Oh, but you will," he said.

Then, in a flash, the resemblance struck me. "You look just like Wayne," I said, mentioning my sister Ruth Ann's husband.

"Yup. That's my dad," George said. "Or, he will be."

"When are you coming?" I asked, anxious to know.

"Soon," George said, his smile fading. "But listen. If you get your memories back, please tell Mom and Dad that I'm going to be all right, and that I'm a missionary."

I put my hand out and fingered a lapel on his suit. "You certainly look the part," I said, hoping to see him smile again. "You're only missing one thing."

George tipped his head at me. "What?"

"Your nametag," I said with a full-blown smile, dimples and all.

George rewarded me with the grin I'd hoped for. "Don't you worry, Aunt Suzie, that will all be taken care of."

David George Stewart did come one year later, on November 28, 2000. He only stayed for three hours before he went back to heaven. I've no doubt that he's immersed in missionary work, and I look forward to greeting him again some day.

It's so important to know that our loved ones on the other side are happy, and they're not very far from us. We can take comfort knowing that they are with us when we need them if we just ask. When we grieve for someone, we're really grieving for ourselves, because the ones who have passed do not want us to dwell on their death. If you do, they won't stay in your presence, because they want us to remember them in happy times.

Before I returned to my body, we had a going away party, attended by Helaman's army and the Stripling Warriors along with my family and every new and old friend I had made.

There was a big feast with tables as laden as a medieval banquet. Every conceivable food was there, laid out on long tables with white tablecloths and beautiful centerpieces. I couldn't help but wonder if a heavenly florist had made the centerpieces. Again, it was whispered to my mind that we do what we like to do in heaven.

Fruits and vegetables of every shape and size, some I had never seen before, rested in various bowls, and there was energy shaped and flavored like turkey for the taking. We ate and ate. I love eating in heaven because there is no guilt and you never get too full.

Then the music started. I looked up, delighted with the sound of old ballroom dance tunes. I ended up dancing with practically everyone, steps like the fox trot and the waltz. There was also singing, with several people taking center stage and doing karaoke-type songs.

When Christ took his turn on stage, he sang the Primary song, "I Wonder When He Comes Again." He performed it as a ballad, in a wonderfully mellow and deep voice, with perfect pitch. He put his whole heart into it. I thought it was kind of funny that he was singing a song about himself, so I laughed, but not with the intent to make fun of him. I was simply delighted with his performance. When I laughed, he laughed, too, but kept on singing until the song was through. He knew my heart, and he was okay with my laughter.

The last dance I had was with Christ. Since he is perfect, then of course he is a great dancer, too. He knows how to teach a new dance step in a way that is easily understood, even by someone like me! He even dipped me once!

Christ sang along with the song in his perfect voice, and I could see why just being around him on earth made some people crazy. They couldn't stand how good he was at everything. They let their jealousy get the best of them, and that let Satan in, and they handed their hearts over to him to do with as he wished. If instead of seeing Christ as flaunting his perfection before them, they could have seen him as inviting them to join him while loving them all along the way, they would have had a different point of view.

If you're angry, it invites evil into your life. Not only does anger invite evil, but it comes in through improper thoughts, music, videos, books, and movies, too.

Some spirits are "homebound," meaning they stay on this earthly plane because they don't realize they have passed away. Even if other spirits tell them they're dead, these homebound spirits must choose whether or not to believe it.

Most of the homebound spirits aren't here for any good purpose. Some don't want to look up, and some may not even know how to look up and see the light. Even in my own instance, when I was in the operating room and found myself floating against the ceiling, I only looked down at my body, with my thoughts focused solely on my children and their earthly welfare. If I had bothered to look up, I would have seen Christ before he had to get my attention by taking hold of my arm.

Some homebound spirits may be selfish, or so attached to their earthly things that they don't want to leave them. In basic physics, you learn about molecular vibration. All energy has a vibrational level, and some things vibrate faster than others, sort of like varying wavelengths of different colors of light. If you're thinking more of earthly things than heavenly things, it keeps your vibrations lower and you're not on a heavenly plane.

After the dance, it was time for me to go. Although the measurement of time in heaven is completely different than time on earth, I had to get back before a certain earthly time elapsed. My family members hugged me goodbye amid tears of joy and words of encouragement about my return to mortality. I hugged people all around me, and several of my relatives promised to help me and watch over my family.

I cried, because the hardest thing I have ever had to do or will ever have to do was to leave that beautiful place. In spite of the hole in my heart, I still knew that I was doing the right thing. It's a good thing for me that I had already made the choice to stay with my children on earth, because if not for that commitment, then I'm afraid I might have chosen to remain in heaven.

Christ led me by the hand back to the operating room. My body was still on the surgery table. I could hear the doctors say, "She's not breathing." There was general chaos, and I could see the people below me with defribulator paddles poised, getting ready to shock me back to life.

"Never forget that I love you," Jesus said. I turned toward him and saw that his eyes were wet with tears. Tears spilled down my cheeks. It was so hard to leave him.

Christ is an amazing being. Even though he's a respected and beloved figure in heaven and to many people on earth, he doesn't put out any expectations that he's better than any body else, never. Nobody holds a higher station, yet he's the most humble of us all. People flock to him simply because they want to, not because they're forced to do so.

We are told that no calling is greater than another.

The Lord doesn't consider himself as better than anyone else, and neither do the people in heaven. They all came out to meet me because they liked what I had done, not because they wanted to impress me with how great they were. No one is greater than another in the sight of the Lord. He loves us all the same. He's disappointed when we do wrong, and sometimes he sends a lightning bolt in our direction as a warning, but that's only because he loves us.

"Remember I will always be with you." The resonance of Christ's compassionate voice echoed in my soul as he kissed me on my cheek. In an instant, I was back inside my body, where the operating room staff appeared to be moving in fast motion. I gasped, drawing in the breath of life.

CHAPTER 17

Remembering

As promised, the memories of my time spent in heaven were taken from me. My recovery from the ectopic pregnancy was slow, but complete. I was despondent in the recovery room, feeling completely helpless. After all, the doctors had removed my unborn baby from me.

When James got home a couple of days later, he wondered if the doctors couldn't have reimplanted the baby into my uterus, but it was too late. The embryo was already dead.

My sisters Merrianne and Ruth Ann took care of my children for about three weeks. Once I was back on my feet and home again, I had to deal with my friend Pam being pregnant, and my sister Merrianne being due three days after I had been. Without knowing why at the time, when I got the news that Merrianne had given birth to a baby girl, it felt as through my heart was shredded. I cried out my grief, and found underneath it a quiet joy that my sister's baby had arrived alive and well.

This was a difficult time in my life. Recovery was long, and I was constantly tired for three months straight. I had a lump on my side for six months, and the doctor told me that my fallopian tube was scarred and useless.

Over time I settled into routine life with my husband and children. A year and a half later we welcomed little Wesley Hyrum into our family.

It was around that time that my husband was involved in a serious truck accident in Tooele, Utah. As soon as I heard about it, my heart pounded with worry, even though I soon learned that he wasn't seriously hurt. If circumstances had been slightly different, he could have been killed. What would we ever do without him? If he was on the other side of the veil, out of my reach, then I'd be left alone to raise our children.

As I drove toward Tooele to pick him up, my thoughts about what could have happened shifted my worry by degrees along a sliding scale of emotions until it touched on the red band of anger. I never slipped into true anger, not in the sense that people sometimes feel abandoned and unreasonably angry toward a loved one who dies and leaves them behind.

Mine was more a feeling of intense worry interspersed with incredible sadness. The accident brought the question up close and personal: what would I do if James had really died and left me to live my life without him? If anyone were to go, I would rather it be me. I wanted to live in heaven, where it seemed from some shadow of a memory that it would be so beautiful it almost hurt your eyes, and so tranquil that sitting under a tree could infuse you with peaceful energy.

After I picked up James and assured myself that he really was all right, I drove toward home, thinking what an adventure it would be to actually see the other side.

At that moment, for a split second, I saw Christ standing in front of a pure white background with his arm around a man who looked like James. Someone else moved forward to shake James' hand. I blinked, and the image was gone. I didn't tell James what I saw. He had endured enough drama for one day.

My mind flitted back to the ectopic pregnancy that I'd suffered, and the long recovery from surgery. But in between there, from the time I was taken to the surgery room until I woke up numb and groggy in recovery, wasn't there something else? I tried to remember the anesthesiologist putting the mask over my face, but the memory eluded me. Yet I had to have been put under in order for them to perform the necessary surgery. I suddenly wanted to remember the details of the time that seemed to be missing. I wanted to fill in the gap that spanned my last conscious thought until I woke up with the promise of biting pain and achingly empty arms.

I found myself pondering the question with increasing frequency, wondering about it while I switched laundry from the washer to the dryer or sat down to nurse Wesley. My little son would sometimes search my face with his dark eyes, then give me a knowing grin before he settled down to eat.

Sometimes I would mention something that I thought I had read in a near-death book to one of my friends or family, and they would say, "I've never heard that before. What book was that?" and I couldn't remember.

In June of 2003 I began to suspect that the things I was remembering and talking about had been my own experiences. Truth comes to those who seek it, and if you don't seek for knowledge, then you won't learn anything. I became a seeker.

There were a lot of things I didn't remember all at once. It was like I'd taken a vacation and now that I'd been back for awhile, I could remember things I did in bits and pieces but not always in the proper sequence. Sometimes something that someone said in passing would trigger a new memory.

I began praying to have my memories restored.

After asking that the adversary be kept away so that he couldn't influence my memories, I would write down everything that came to mind, and in the writing, more memories came to light.

When I remembered my interactions with BrookLynn Rose, my heart caught and I couldn't stop the tears. I found myself staring at my niece, Rachel, who was the same age that Brook would have been. Rachel happens to have dimples like mine. She also resembles my other daughters so much that I couldn't help but imagine how she and Brook would have played together if Brook had lived.

Eventually, I had enough events in a logical order that I felt like I could tell my husband what I remembered from the moment I died on the surgery table.

As I spoke, he raised his eyebrows in disbelief. "I've heard this before."

"No, you haven't. It happened to me while I was in the hospital and you were on the road."

"But I know this story," he insisted.

After we discussed it at length, the best thing we could figure out is that since James and I were married in the temple, then on a subconscious level, his spirit did indeed know what my spirit was doing and where it had gone during the time I was out of my body. Since we're eternally sealed, his spirit knew what mine was up to.

I had always thought that I would die young. I often wonder if I changed my future by choosing to come back.

The feeling that I needed to get my story out to others grew stronger with each passing day, but I resisted the impulse because I didn't want to be viewed as weird or as anyone who thought she was more important than anyone else. Still, the feeling persisted.

One evening I was enjoying the rare treat of soaking in the bathtub late at night. I sank down to my chin in bubbles, trying to clear my mind of every chore I hadn't yet finished and every task that I had to tackle the next day. I was doing a pretty good job of it, probably the result of sheer exhaustion, when a thought broke through my stupor. *Get your story out.*

I wrinkled my brow. *"But I don't want people to think I'm a weirdo."*

The answer to my worry was unmistakable. *"Then don't act like one."*

Scripture References

After my return from Paradise, the scriptures came alive for me. Truths that I had overlooked before my experience now jumped out at me, and their importance was magnified. In conclusion, I would like to share some of the many references that are dear to my heart and hopefully will have meaning in your life.

Deuteronomy 4:29—*But if from thence thou shalt seek the LORD thy God, thou shalt find him, if thou seek him with all thy heart and with all thy soul.*

Abraham 1:18—*Behold, I will lead thee by my hand, and I will take thee, to put upon thee my name, even the Priesthood of thy father, and my power shall be over thee.*

Mark 10:13-16—*And they brought young children to him, that he should touch them: and his disciples rebuked those that brought them.*

But when Jesus saw it, he was much displeased, and said unto them, Suffer the little children to come unto me, and forbid them not: for of such is the kingdom of God.

Verily I say unto you, Whosoever shall not receive

the kingdom of God as a little child, he shall not enter therein.

And he took them up in his arms, put his hands upon them, and blessed them.

John 10:14—*I am the good shepherd, and know my sheep, and am known of mine.*

John 10:27-28—*My sheep hear my voice, and I know them, and they follow me: And I give unto them eternal life; and they shall never perish, neither shall any man pluck them out of my hand.*

James 1:5—*If any of you lack wisdom, let him ask of God, that giveth to all men liberally, and upbraideth not; and it shall be given him.*

Revelation 2:7—*He that hath an ear, let him hear what the Spirit saith unto the churches; To him that overcometh will I give to eat of the tree of life, which is in the midst of the paradise of God.*

Alma 32:21—*And now as I said concerning faith— faith is not to have a perfect knowledge of things; therefore if ye have faith ye hope for things which are not seen, which are true.*

Alma 40:11-14—*Now, concerning the state of the soul between death and the resurrection—Behold, it has been made known unto me by an angel, that the spirits of all men, as soon as they are departed from this mortal body, yea, the spirits of all men, whether they be good or evil, are taken home to that God who gave them life.*

And then shall it come to pass, that the spirits of those who are righteous are received into a state of happiness, which is called paradise, a state of rest, a state of peace, where they shall rest from all their troubles and from all care, and sorrow.

And then shall it come to pass, that the spirits of the wicked, yea, who are evil—for behold, they have no part nor portion of the Spirit of the Lord; for behold, they chose evil works rather than good; therefore the spirit of the devil did enter into them, and take possession of their house—and these shall be cast out into outer darkness; there shall be weeping, and wailing, and gnashing of teeth, and this because of their own iniquity, being led captive by the will of the devil.

Now this is the state of the souls of the wicked, yea, in darkness, and a state of awful, fearful looking for the fiery indignation of the wrath of God upon them; thus they remain in this state, as well as the righteous in paradise, until the time of their resurrection.

Moroni 8:10-12—*Behold I say unto you that this thing shall ye teach—repentance and baptism unto those who are accountable and capable of committing sin; yea, teach parents that they must repent and be baptized, and humble themselves as their little children, and they shall all be saved with their little children.*

And their little children need no repentance, neither baptism. Behold, baptism is unto repentance to the fulfilling the commandments unto the remission of sins.

But little children are alive in Christ, even from the foundation of the world; if not so, God is a partial God, and also a changeable God, and a respecter to persons; for how many little children have died without baptism!

Doctrine & Covenants 6:7—*Seek not for riches but for wisdom, and behold, the mysteries of God shall be unfolded unto you, and then shall you be made rich. Behold, he that hath eternal life is rich.*

Doctrine & Covenants 6:13—*If thou wilt do good, yea, and hold out faithful to the end, thou shalt be saved in the kingdom of God, which is the greatest of all the gifts of God; for there is no gift greater than the gift of salvation.*

Doctrine & Covenants 76:10—*For by my Spirit will I enlighten them, and by my power will I make known unto them the secrets of my will—yea, even those things which eye has not seen, nor ear heard, nor yet entered into the heart of man.*

Doctrine & Covenants 93:1—*Verily, thus saith the Lord: It shall come to pass that every soul who forsaketh his sins and cometh unto me, and calleth on my name, and obeyeth my voice, and keepeth my commandments, shall see my face and know that I am.*

Doctrine & Covenants 137:10—*And I also beheld that all children who die before they arrive at the years of accountability are saved in the celestial kingdom of heaven.*

Doctrine & Covenants 138:55-56—*I observed that they were among the noble and great ones who were chosen in the beginning to be rulers in the Church of God.*

Even before they were born, they, with many others, received their first lessons in the world of spirits and were prepared to come forth in the due time of the Lord to labor in his vineyard for the salvation of the souls of men.

About Suzanne Freeman

Suzanne Scholes Freeman began her adventure as a mother with her marriage to James Freeman on October 14, 1983. Together, they have been blessed with nine children.

Suzanne loves to cook, and is especially good at baking bread. Her cooking talent expanded into a one-time business of creating her own mixes. She still tries out new recipes which blesses her family's dinner hour.

Suzanne can also piece a quilt and sew from patterns she has made up herself. She enjoys this creative hobby, and creating beautiful things brings her joy. Best of all, she loves to watch her children grow.

You can contact Suzanne through her publisher, at **public_relations@springcreekbooks.com** to arrange speaking opportunities.

About Shirley Bahlmann

Shirley Anderson Bahlmann is the author of several volumes of true pioneer stories, *Against All Odds, Isn't That Odd, Even Love Is Odd,* and *Unseen Odds.*

Shirley also has a published novel entitled *Walker's Gold,* with the sequels *Fool's Gold* and *Bands of Gold* in the works.

She is the wife of award-winning sports writer Bob Bahlmann and they are the parents of six sons. Please visit her website at www.shirleybahlmann.com to see her writing tips and learn more about her upcoming books.